OTTER IN THE OUTHOUSE

'You mean that if Mr Tarrant's plan goes ahead our family of otters could die?' asked Mandy, horrified.

Rosie nodded. 'They certainly couldn't remain on Loch Ferran. I don't know where else they could go.'

'But that's terrible,' Mandy protested. 'Can't we do *anything* about it?'

Rosie's mouth set in a firm line. 'I'm certainly going to try,' she said. 'I'm going to have a word with Mr "Watersports" Tarrant!'

Animal Ark series

LUCY DANIELS

Otter
— *in the* —
Outhouse

Illustrations by Jenny Gregory

Hodder
Children's
Books

a division of Hodder Headline plc

Special thanks to Helen Magee
Thanks also to C. J. Hall, B.Vet.Med., M.R.C.V.S., for reviewing
the veterinary information contained in this book.

Text copyright © 1998 Ben M. Baglio
Created by Ben M. Baglio, London W12 7QY
Illustrations copyright © 1998 Jenny Gregory

First published in Great Britain in 1998
by Hodder Children's Books

A Catalogue record for this book is available from the British Library

ISBN 0 340 69955 8

Typeset by Avon Dataset Ltd, Bidford-on-Avon, Warks

Printed and bound in Great Britain by
Clays Ltd, St Ives plc

Hodder Children's Books
a division of Hodder Headline plc
338 Euston Road
London NW1 3BH

One

'There she is! There's Rosie!' Mandy Hope said to James Hunter excitedly.

James shoved his glasses up on his nose and shifted the weight of his rucksack. 'Where?' he asked.

'There!' Mandy pointed to a young woman with short dark hair and brown eyes. She looked fit and tanned. 'She's waving to us. Come on, James.'

Mandy headed across the arrivals hall at Glasgow airport. Rosie was amongst a crowd of people waiting to meet the passengers off the plane. She smiled broadly as Mandy and James approached.

'Rosie!' Mandy called.

'It's good to see you,' Rosie said to Mandy, shaking her hand warmly. 'How was the journey?'

'Terrific,' said Mandy. She pushed her short fair hair out of her eyes. 'Dad took us to the airport at Leeds. He was going to a conference there so it was quite convenient for him. Flying was great fun!'

'We had a *nanny!*' James said disgustedly.

Mandy laughed. 'It was only a stewardess,' she explained. 'All she did was see that we got the plane to Glasgow and not Paris or somewhere. They have to do that if you're under twelve.'

Mandy was twelve and James, her best friend, was a year younger. Mandy knew that he was annoyed because he felt the nanny had been for him.

James grunted. 'It was embarrassing.'

'Hi, James,' Rosie said, her dark eyes twinkling. 'How's Blackie?'

Blackie was James's black Labrador. He normally went everywhere with James. 'I don't think he was very pleased at being left behind,' James replied. 'But Dad has promised to walk him twice a day while I'm away.'

'Just think how glad he'll be to see you when you get back,' said Rosie. 'And, by the way, don't worry. I won't be doing any nannying while you're at Ardferran. You two are going to be my *colleagues.*'

James grinned. 'That sounds a lot better,' he said. 'Colleagues! I like that.'

Mandy smiled. She and James were going to Ardferran on the west coast of Scotland to help Rosie with her wildlife project – a survey of otters in the area. Rosie Driver was a young Scottish friend of Mandy's parents, who were vets in her home village of Welford, in Yorkshire. Mr and Mrs Hope worked at Animal Ark, the surgery attached to their cottage. Rosie had once done a placement at Animal Ark while she was studying ecology and wildlife preservation at university. She had remained great friends with Mandy's parents – and with Mandy.

'I can't wait to see the otters,' Mandy said.

'Let's get going then,' Rosie said. 'We've still got a three-hour journey by car.'

'Three hours?' said Mandy as she and James followed Rosie out of the foyer doors and into the carpark. 'It doesn't look that far on the map.'

'It isn't so very far as the crow flies,' said Rosie. 'But the road is really winding. We have to go round a whole series of lochs, or lakes, as you call them in England,' said Rosie, half-smiling. The whole of the west coast of Scotland is dotted with lochs. A great many of them are sea lochs, like Loch Ferran where we're going.'

'Does that mean they're tidal?' asked Mandy.

Rosie nodded. 'They're inlets from the sea,' she explained. 'Some of them are very long, like Loch Ferran. If you imagine a long finger of seawater stretching inland, you've got the picture.'

'So do otters like seawater?' James asked.

Rosie nodded again. 'They especially like sea lochs,' she said. 'Sea lochs are protected from the open sea but at the same time there are lots of fish and crabs to catch. It's the perfect habitat for otters. They love playing in the seaweed.'

'Will we be able to go and look at them straight away?' asked Mandy as Rosie stopped in front of a red car. It looked a bit battered and dusty.

Rosie looked at her watch. 'We might catch a glimpse of them at dusk.'

'But it'll be after nine by the time we get there,' James said.

Rosie opened the car boot and laughed. 'It stays light enough to read a book outside until after eleven o'clock,' she said. 'You'll be amazed at how long the light lasts up there in summer.'

'Wow!' exclaimed James. 'It sounds a fantastic place.'

'It's worth the long drive, I can tell you,' Rosie replied. 'You'll love Ardferran.'

Mandy tossed her rucksack into the boot beside James's.

'It sounds like heaven,' she said, climbing into the back seat of the car.

Rosie slammed the boot shut and got into the driving seat. 'Otter heaven!' she said.

As Rosie drove off, Mandy settled back and thought about the series of events that had led to her and James coming to Scotland. Rosie had been working on the otter project all summer. She was completing a postgraduate degree and this project was the most important work she had ever done. Then disaster had struck when Julie, her co-worker, had broken her leg and had to go home.

'How is your friend?' Mandy asked.

'She's in plaster up to her hip,' Rosie said. 'Poor Julie. She's really disappointed at not being able to complete the work – but she says to be sure and tell you how grateful she is to you and James for helping me out.'

'We're going to love it,' James insisted. 'I'm really glad Mandy came up with the idea.'

'And I'm glad I phoned your mum to tell her the bad news last week,' Rosie said to Mandy. 'I was at my wits' end. I've only got a week left. I'd never finish in time on my own.'

'Mum said it was important that you got all your results in,' said Mandy.

Rosie nodded as she turned out of the airport and on to the motorway. 'I'm hoping to present them to a wildlife trust. Maybe they'll be good enough to win me funding for more research. Maybe even a job at a wildlife centre.'

'Is that what you want to do?' asked James.

Rosie nodded again. 'More than anything in the world,' she replied. 'It's my dream. And you two are going to help it come true.'

'I *hope* we can,' said Mandy seriously. 'We've brought notebooks and binoculars and we've read everything we could about otters.'

'We didn't have much time though,' said James. 'I've never even seen an otter.'

'I saw an otter in Jura,' Mandy chipped in. 'But that was in a river, not a sea loch.'

'Does that mean the otters we're going to study are sea otters?' James asked.

Rosie shook her head. 'No,' she explained. 'They're river otters, just like the one Mandy saw. We don't have sea otters in Britain. They're much bigger – quite different from our otters at Ardferran. They live most of their lives at sea and hardly ever come ashore. The otters *we're* studying are *Lutra lutra* or common otters.'

'It sounds complicated,' said James.

'It isn't really,' said Rosie. She smiled. 'Remember when I was doing my placement at Animal Ark two years ago and you helped me with the vole count?'

James nodded. 'Water voles,' he replied. He screwed up his face. '*Arvicola terrestris.*'

'Well done, James,' said Rosie. 'Fancy you remembering their Latin name.'

James blushed and shoved his brown floppy hair back off his eyes. 'At least *Lutra lutra* is easier to say than *Arvicola terrestris*,' he said.

'Water vole is even easier,' Mandy remarked. 'We found loads of them. It was really interesting, watching them.'

'I want you to do the same kind of thing at Ardferran,' Rosie said.

'You mean count them?' asked Mandy.

'There are only six,' Rosie said. 'A dog otter, two bitches and three cubs.'

'Cubs!' exclaimed Mandy. 'How lovely.'

'What I want you to help me to do is track their movements,' Rosie went on. 'Otters are creatures of habit – if they aren't disturbed. So that makes it easier to track them. Unfortunately for us, they're also extremely good at camouflage. You can sit for ages looking at a patch of seaweed and it's only when the otter moves that you realise it's been there all along.'

'So we have to be very quiet,' said Mandy.

'It's just as well I didn't bring Blackie,' James put in. 'He would want to play with them.'

'Oh, no, he wouldn't,' Rosie said. 'Otters have a very nasty bite. I think Blackie would keep well out of their way.'

'But they look so gorgeous,' Mandy protested.

Rosie smiled. 'Wait till you see them feeding and get a look at the dog otter's teeth. They're wild animals after all.'

'Of course,' Mandy agreed.

'If you want something to cuddle there are four kittens at the cottage,' said Rosie. 'They love a cuddle.'

'Kittens!' Mandy cried. 'You didn't tell us that when you phoned.'

'I had other things on my mind when I phoned,' Rosie said with a sigh.

'But who do the kittens belong to?' James asked. 'Are they yours?'

Rosie made a face. 'I suppose they are,' she said. 'But what on earth I'm supposed to do with four kittens and a mother cat at the end of this week I just don't know.'

'Where did you get them?' asked Mandy.

'I found the mother cat in the outhouse about six weeks ago,' Rosie informed her. 'She had just given birth. I've no idea where she came from. It's obvious she's used to people, but there isn't anybody else around for miles.'

'I thought the cottage was on an estate,' Mandy said. 'Isn't there a big house?'

'There is,' said Rosie. 'But it's been empty for nearly two months now. The previous owners went abroad. Mr Tarrant, the new owner, is supposed to be moving in this week.'

'Maybe the mother cat belonged to the people that were there before,' James suggested. 'Do you think they just abandoned it when they went away?'

Mandy nodded. 'That's probably what happened. People can be so cruel sometimes. They probably didn't want all the bother of a litter of kittens.'

'I haven't had time to make enquiries,' said Rosie. 'We're so isolated at the cottage and I've been so busy.'

'Don't worry about it,' Mandy reassured her. 'We'll find out who the cat belongs to – and the kittens.'

'I'll certainly be glad of a hand with them,' said Rosie. 'Those kittens are beginning to get everywhere. Sometimes it seems like forty, not just four.'

Mandy grinned. 'What have you called them?' she asked.

Rosie laughed. 'I haven't got round to that yet,' she replied. 'I've called the mother cat Ferran because I found her near Loch Ferran. I tell you what – you can name the kittens.'

'Great,' Mandy enthused. 'I can't wait to see them.'

'You're going to be busy,' warned Rosie. 'Otters *and* kittens.'

'I know about kittens,' Mandy said, 'but there's so much to learn about otters.'

'You'll be fine,' said Rosie. 'But there will be a lot of watching and waiting and taking notes. I hope you won't be bored sitting on a rock for an hour waiting for the otters to appear.'

'Bored!' Mandy was scandalised. 'How could we be bored with kittens to look after and otters to watch?'

Rosie laughed. 'You haven't changed since two years ago, Mandy,' she said.

James grinned. 'Mandy will never change,' he stated firmly. 'For Mandy, animals will always be the most important things in the world.'

Two

'This is Camus Ferran,' announced Rosie, looking round the little bay on the edge of Loch Ferran. 'Camus is Gaelic for "bay".'

'So it's Ferran Bay in English,' said James. He put his head on one side. 'I think Camus Ferran sounds nicer.'

'The cottage is called Ferran Cottage,' Rosie went on. 'What do you think of it?'

Mandy put her rucksack down thankfully and looked at the two-storey, white-painted cottage. A stream ran down from the hills behind and flowed into the loch. A rowing-boat was drawn up on the beach below the cottage.

The road had stopped half a mile from the cottage and they had left the car at the top of the track. But the view in front of them made the walk worthwhile. The cottage nestled at the foot of a low hill on a slight rise, not far from the water's edge. There was a perfect semicircle of beach in front of it with a scattering of rocks and, behind it, a belt of trees.

'Oh, look at those birds,' Mandy exclaimed, pointing to the beach. 'Aren't they funny?'

A whole crowd of little birds scurried up the beach as a wave came in. Once the wave receded, they raced back down towards the water, only to scamper back again ahead of the next wave.

'Those are ringed plovers,' James informed her. He was a keen birdwatcher.

'They look as if they don't want to get their feet wet,' said Mandy, laughing. She looked around. 'This is perfect.'

'I'm going to have a lot to put into my bird-spotting record,' James enthused, shading his eyes and gazing out across the loch.

Loch Ferran was a long, narrow sea loch, dotted with tiny islands. Some of the islands had stands of trees growing on them. Others were rocky and bare.

'There must be about ten islands out there,' Mandy guessed.

'Some of them are hardly big enough to be called islands,' Rosie said. 'They're just outcrops of rock. Do you like it?'

'It looks wonderful,' breathed Mandy as a flock of birds rose into the air and wheeled across the water. 'What are those?'

'Oyster-catchers,' replied Rosie.

James had his binoculars out, trained on the flight of birds swooping low over the loch. Mandy fished hers out of her rucksack and got the birds in sight.

As she watched, the birds heeled hard against the sky.

'There are so many of them.' Mandy shook her head wonderingly. 'What a marvellous place.'

'I'm glad you like it,' Rosie said. 'I do too – in spite of the walk. I have to collect my delivery of eggs, milk and post from outside Ardferran House.'

'Where's that?' asked Mandy.

'We passed the gates just where the track to Camus Ferran turned off,' Rosie told her.

Mandy remembered seeing tall stone gates. 'It must be a huge house,' she remarked.

'Pretty big,' agreed Rosie. 'But it needs a lot of work. Mr Tarrant has got a big job in front of him. He's going to build a proper road down to Camus Ferran too and renovate the cottage. That's why I have to leave at the end of this week.'

'Is he going to live there all on his own?' Mandy asked.

Rosie shrugged. 'I'm not sure. All I know is that he agreed to let the project continue after the last owners left. That was really all I was interested in.'

'I'd like to see the house,' Mandy said.

'You don't have to go by the track,' Rosie said. 'There's a shortcut through the woods.'

'We'll collect the milk and stuff tomorrow morning,' James offered. 'Save you a trip.'

'That would be great. Thanks, James,' Rosie said gratefully. 'Then you can go and have a look at the house.'

'Wouldn't Mr Tarrant mind?' asked Mandy.

'I don't think he's there yet,' Rosie replied. She narrowed her eyes and pointed out towards the loch.

'What is it?' enquired Mandy.

'Look!' Rosie exclaimed. 'That's Eilean Mor, the big island with the trees. See the rocks at the water's edge? There's the dog otter.'

Mandy and James raised their binoculars. Mandy was so excited she could hardly hold them steady. Then she got the otter in sight. It had sleek dark brown fur and small rounded ears. It was sitting on a rock but it wasn't sitting still. It was twisting about.

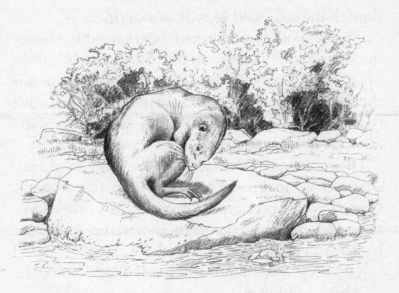

'What's it doing?' asked Mandy.

'He's grooming himself,' said Rosie. 'Otters spend hours every day cleaning their fur. It's hard work because their fur is so thick but they have to do it.'

'Why is it so important?' James asked.

'Their coats are waterproof,' Rosie replied. 'But if they get dirty they lose their resistance to water and the otter gets wet and quite literally catches cold. Otters are mammals, remember. They're warm-blooded so they need protection from the cold and wet.'

'And yet the otters at Ardferran spend so much

time in the sea,' said Mandy wonderingly.

'That's another reason our otters need to clean their fur a lot,' Rosie went on. 'Salt crystals build up on their coats. If they didn't get rid of them their fur would get tangled. Usually an otter will try to find a freshwater pool to wash off the salt after it's been in the sea.'

They watched, fascinated, as the otter used his sharp claws to groom his fur. Then the animal twisted, rolled over on the ground a few times and slipped from the rock into the water. It did a backward flip and disappeared.

'Oh, it's gone,' Mandy groaned, disappointed.

'Wait,' said Rosie.

Mandy held her breath. There was a flurry of water and the dog otter appeared again, swimming for the shore. It had something in its mouth.

'What has it got?' asked James.

Rosie screwed up her eyes. 'It's hard to tell from this distance but it's probably an eel by the size of it.'

Mandy watched as the otter dragged its food up on to the shore and bit into it, holding the eel in its paws and tearing at the flesh with sharp teeth.

'Wow!' she said. 'I see what you mean about the teeth.'

In no time at all, the otter had finished eating

the eel. He slid back into the water, but this time he wasn't hunting. He lay lazily on his back, drifting with the tide. 'He looks as if he's having an after-dinner snooze,' laughed James.

Then, with an incredibly swift movement, the otter disappeared, leaving only spreading ripples on the surface of the water.

Rosie opened the door to the cottage. 'Come and see your rooms,' she said. 'They're pretty basic but the views are terrific.'

'Do you think the otter will come back?' asked Mandy, unwilling to leave.

'He might,' said Rosie. 'But I think we should get you two settled in. You can always go down to the shore later. Besides, I have a hungry mother cat to feed.'

'And the kittens,' Mandy added. 'I'd forgotten all about them.'

'I wouldn't mind having something to eat,' James said. 'I haven't eaten for hours.'

'Poor James,' Rosie sympathised. 'You must be starving.'

'James is *always* starving,' Mandy asserted as they followed Rosie through the door and into the cottage.

The door opened straight into the living-room. Mandy's eyes went immediately to a blue plastic box. A black-and-white cat poked her head over the edge of the box, yawned and began to purr. Nestled against her were four little bundles of fur: the kittens.

'Oh, aren't they gorgeous!' Mandy murmured, going over to the box and bending down.

'Two boys and two girls,' Rosie told her.

Mandy put out a hand to let the mother cat sniff her fingers, then she stroked one of the kittens gently. The mother cat mewed but didn't seem alarmed. The box was lined with an old, soft blanket.

'That's a fishing crate I found on the shore,' explained Rosie. 'It was the best I could do for them.'

'It's a perfect bed,' said Mandy. 'And she has four perfect kittens.'

Rosie went to the fridge and rummaged for milk. Then she put some cat food into a bowl and set it down on the floor beside the box. The mother cat leaped nimbly for it, leaving her kittens mewing after her.

'There, there,' whispered Mandy, picking one up. 'She'll be back in a minute. She's just gone to have her dinner. She'll be back to feed you.'

'They're almost weaned,' Rosie said. 'They should be big enough to leave Ferran soon.'

'It's a lovely name,' said Mandy.

'I thought so too,' said Rosie, looking fondly at Ferran. 'I just don't know what I'm going to do at the end of the week.'

Mandy gave the kitten a kiss on its tiny nose and put it back in the box with the others.

'We'll think of something,' she promised.

Ferran polished off the remains of her dinner, gave herself a quick wash and stepped delicately back into the box. The kittens clustered round, nudging at one another, trying to get close to their mother as they took turns to suckle.

'That's the animals fed,' said Rosie. 'Now, why don't I show you your rooms and then rustle us up something to eat while you two get unpacked.'

'Brilliant,' cried James. 'Come on, Mandy.'

Mandy and James followed Rosie up the little staircase to the top floor. The bedrooms were tiny. Each had a bed, a chest of drawers and a rug on the sanded wooden floor. There wasn't room for much else. But the views from the windows were just as good as Rosie had promised.

'These are gorgeous,' Mandy enthused, running between the two rooms.

Rosie grinned. 'I'll leave you to sort out who's having which,' she said as she went back downstairs.

'Which one do you want?' asked James, going to

get his rucksack from the landing where he had dumped it.

Mandy looked out of the bedroom window. From here she could see right out across the loch. She opened the little window and poked her head out. She had a view of the woods and the stream running down past the cottage. 'This one,' she said. 'It's perfect.'

'They're both perfect,' James replied, dragging his rucksack into the other room. 'I can see all the islands if I stick my head right out of the window – and I've got a great view of the shore. Race you to unpack!'

James finished unpacking in double-quick time and sat by Mandy's window as she folded her things and put them away. Every so often his nose would twitch as the smells of cooking drifted upstairs.

'Ready,' said Mandy at last.

James was staring out of the window. 'Mandy,' he breathed, 'I think I've just seen an eagle.'

He dashed into his bedroom and came out with his bird book, flicking through the pages.

But when they went downstairs Rosie didn't think it had been an eagle.

'More likely a buzzard,' she suggested as she put a Spanish omelette in front of each of them. There was a big bowl of salad and a loaf of crusty bread too. 'If you're lucky you might see an osprey,' she went on. 'I've seen one around Ardferran from time to time.'

'An osprey!' cried James. 'Wow!'

'What else will we see at Ardferran?' Mandy asked eagerly. 'Will we see deer?'

'Not at this time of year,' Rosie replied. 'They'll all be up in the hills for the summer feeding. But there are pine martens. Pine martens belong to the same family as stoats and weasels but you don't often catch sight of them. You'll love watching the birds on Loch Ferran, James. Oyster-catchers, cormorants and all kinds of divers.'

Mandy listened as Rosie and James discussed birds. But her mind was full of the dog otter they had sighted. She couldn't wait to see him again.

'That was wonderful,' James said, sitting back and patting his stomach.

Mandy scraped the last of the omelette off her plate and nibbled on a lettuce leaf.

'Mmm,' she agreed. 'You're a terrific cook, Rosie.'

Rosie started gathering up plates. 'Thank you,' she replied.

'The kittens are well fed too,' remarked James, looking at the fishing box. Ferran had settled down to sleep and so had her kittens.

'Poor little scraps,' Mandy said. 'We'll just *have* to find homes for them.'

'And soon,' added Rosie, taking the dirty plates to the sink. 'We've only got a week.'

Mandy frowned. 'Do you think they'd let me on the plane with a basketful of kittens – and Ferran?'

James looked at her in amazement. 'You're not thinking of taking them back to Welford?' he asked.

'We can't leave them here if they don't have homes to go to,' Mandy asserted.

James shook his head. 'What *will* the nanny say?' he said and Mandy grinned.

She didn't care what the nanny would say. She would smuggle the kittens back to Welford if she couldn't find homes for them here in Ardferran.

'Do you want to phone home and let your parents know you arrived safely?' Rosie asked.

Mandy and James nodded. 'I want to tell them all about the otters,' Mandy said, reaching for the phone.

'And I want Mum to look up one of my bird books for me,' James declared. 'That *might* have been an eagle after all.'

Fifteen minutes later Mandy put the phone down. Mr and Mrs Hope had given her a rundown on the progress of all the patients at Animal Ark since she left that morning.

'What about Ginger?' Mandy had asked. Ginger was a hamster who had contracted a skin rash. The poor little thing's fur had been falling out.

'I gave him the all-clear today,' Emily Hope said down the phone. 'The rash has gone and his fur is growing back. He'll soon be as good as new.'

'Great,' said Mandy. 'I was worried about Ginger.'

'Don't worry,' advised her mum. 'Just have a great time.'

'Oh, I will,' Mandy assured her as she rang off. Her mum and dad promised to phone later in the week.

She handed the phone to James and frowned as she remembered something her dad had said when she told him about Rosie's kittens. 'Haven't you got any neighbours that would like a kitten?' he had asked. There must be *some* people in Ardferran, she thought. They couldn't be the only ones around.

Three

'Are you going down to the shore, Mandy?' Rosie asked.

'Don't you want me to help with the washing-up?' Mandy asked.

Rosie shook her head. 'Not on your first night,' she replied. 'But you won't get off so easily after this. Now would be a good time to go. You can usually see one or two of the otters around at this time of night. They like to come out in the late evening when the light is dimming.'

Mandy jumped up. 'Are you coming, James?' she asked.

James shook his head, his eyes focused on

Rosie's small desk by the window. 'I thought I might have a look at the computer,' he said. 'You've got all your data on there, haven't you, Rosie?'

Rosie nodded. 'I need an up-to-date printout. You could do that for me, James.'

James looked surprised. 'Would you trust me?' he asked.

'I've told you,' said Rosie. 'We're colleagues.'

James flushed with pleasure and Mandy smiled as she slipped her anorak on and made for the door. James was mad about computers. Rosie had just made a friend for life.

'I'll come down in a little while, Mandy,' James called after her. 'Where will you be?'

Mandy looked at Rosie enquiringly. 'Where's the best place?' she asked.

'Go down to the shore and round past the bay opposite Eilean Mor,' Rosie told her. 'There are rocks on the shore down there and you just might be lucky. The best spot to watch from is just on the edge of the trees. The wind is off the water so they shouldn't scent you.'

'Would that upset them?' asked Mandy.

Rosie nodded. 'Absolutely,' she said. 'Otters are very quick to scent humans. Just make sure the wind is blowing in your face when you're otter-watching. That way you can be sure they won't catch your scent.'

Mandy stepped out into the night. The lights from the cottage splashed on the ground in front of her and she used their light to scramble down on to the shore. Once down there, the lights disappeared behind the banking and Mandy gasped. The loch was a shining sheet of water, reflecting the soft light from the sky. Mandy looked at her watch. Rosie was right. It was nearly ten o'clock and it was still light.

She walked along the shore, feeling the faint chill of the breeze coming off the water. At first she thought it was completely quiet. Then she began to hear sounds. The lapping of the water on the shore, the faint rustling of the trees behind the beach and, once, the flap of wings as a dark shape rose from the loch and beat a path across its mirror surface down towards the headlands at the end of Loch Ferran out towards the sea. Was it a cormorant flying?

Mandy found the bay and walked as quietly as she could up the shore until she was at the edge of the trees. She lifted her face. Yes, she could feel the faintest trace of a breeze on it. Quietly she sat down and waited, her eyes on the barely rippled waters of the loch. She waited for a long time without moving.

When the otter came, she almost missed it. It glided so silently through the water, hardly disturbing the surface, that she thought at first it was a wavelet caused by the breeze. She strained her eyes. The light was fading a little now and in the half-light she couldn't quite understand the odd humped shape. Then she gave a little gasp as the otter came to the shore and scrambled up on to the rocks.

It was a female otter with a cub on her back. As Mandy watched, the mother otter twisted round and shook the baby off, depositing it on a flat rock. Then, with barely a ripple, she was back in the water and diving. At once, the baby otter set up a piping sound, like a high-pitched squeak.

Moments passed. Mandy bit her lip. The cub seemed to be in distress. Surely the mother otter hadn't abandoned it?

Mandy was almost on the point of moving towards the cub when the female otter reappeared. She had a fish in her mouth. The baby otter must have scented it. It began to scrabble on the rock with its tiny paws but the shrill piping grew weaker. Then the mother scrambled up on the rock and laid the fish in front of her cub.

The mother otter kept hold of the fish with her front paws while the baby bit into it. Mandy watched, fascinated, as the cub sank its tiny teeth into the fish. The mother also tore off chunks and laid them before the cub and, in no time at all, the fish was gone.

Twice more the mother otter slid off the rock and returned, once with a fish and then with what looked like a crab. Mandy couldn't be sure. This time the mother had to feed the food to her cub.

Then the female otter twisted her body under the cub and, in one fluid movement, she was gone, gliding across the still water with the cub a tiny hump on her back.

Mandy watched until the otters merged with the shifting patterns of water. Only then did she look up and realise that it really would soon be dark – properly dark. And out here there were no street-lights. For miles and miles, there was nothing but the dimming sky and the light reflected in the water.

Behind her the trees rustled and Mandy heard the sharp crack of a broken twig. She whirled round. The sound seemed very loud in the still air. 'James?' she said.

There was no answer.

Mandy peered into the trees but it was too dark to make anything out under the overhanging branches. She thought she caught a movement deep in the trees but that could have been her imagination. Maybe it was an animal. Then she heard another crack and a muffled exclamation. It wasn't an animal. Someone was there.

Quickly, Mandy scrambled to her feet and approached the trees. 'James?' she called again.

This time there was an answer. 'Mandy!' said James. But his voice came from the shore, not the trees.

Mandy turned and saw James silhouetted against the light on the water behind him. She crunched her way down to the water's edge. 'There was somebody in the trees,' she told him.

James frowned. 'Who?'

Mandy shook her head. 'I don't know,' she said. 'I thought it was you.'

'I came along the shore,' James replied. 'I wonder who it could have been. Rosie said there wasn't anybody else around for miles.'

Together they walked along the water's edge. 'Obviously there *is* somebody else around,' Mandy remarked. 'We aren't the only ones in Ardferran after all. She paused and grinned. 'Do you think whoever it is would like a kitten?'

James burst out laughing. 'Mandy Hope, you're impossible.'

'It was just a thought.' Mandy began to tell him about the mother otter and her cub.

'I wish I'd seen that,' said James. 'But Rosie's computer files are terrific. She's got charts and graphs of the otters' movements. They really do seem to have a pattern of behaviour. Rosie says otters usually stick to a routine so that makes it quite easy to track them.'

'How do you mean?' asked Mandy.

'There are places they go to each day,' replied James. 'Parts of the shore, the islands. They've got holts in several places.'

Mandy nodded her head. She knew that holts were otters' homes, burrows where they lived and reared their young.

'That should make otter-watching a lot easier,' she said.

James nodded. 'I printed out a couple of charts of their favourite places for us. They're called tracking charts. We can mark the otters' movements on them to build up the pattern even more.'

'It sounds really professional,' Mandy said.

'It is,' agreed James. 'It's for Rosie's project.'

Mandy bit her lip. Of course it was. She had been so taken up with watching the otters for pleasure that she had almost forgotten what a serious purpose it had. Rosie's career could depend on this.

'I'm going to tell her everything I saw just as soon as we get in,' she declared as they headed towards Camus Ferran.

'And I'm going to write up my bird-spotting record,' said James. 'I've got loads to put in it. Look! There's the cottage.'

They could see the lights of the cottage now. They approached the banking and the lights disappeared for a moment. Mandy turned round and looked out over the loch one last time. Ardferran wasn't just otter heaven. It was Mandy Hope heaven too!

James pushed open the cottage door and light flooded out.

Mandy was already talking as she walked through the door, trying to remember every detail for Rosie.

'You were really lucky,' enthused Rosie when she had finished. 'The cubs are too young to fish for themselves yet but the mothers are usually very careful about where they leave them while they go off to fetch dinner. Do you think you could complete a tracking chart for me?'

Mandy nodded eagerly. James was already filling in the record at the back of his bird-spotting book. The cats were still asleep in their box and the cottage was very peaceful.

With Rosie's help, Mandy filled in the chart, writing down exactly what she had seen. There were spaces for various categories. Number of otters. Where seen. Adult/juvenile/cub. Male/female. Activity. Feeding – fish/ crabs/eels/other. Then Rosie gave her a photocopied map of the loch and asked Mandy to circle the precise spot where she'd seen the otters and to put in the time and date.

'This is how I make up my data,' Rosie informed her.

Mandy yawned. 'I can see why you need help,' she said. 'You couldn't do all this on your own.'

Rosie laughed. 'Once you've had some practice otter-watching we'll split up and take different areas. Otters usually have a range of about ten miles and you hardly ever see them all together. The trouble with trying to do it on your own is that you can't be in two places at once.'

Mandy yawned again and Rosie looked guilty. 'Bed for you two,' she declared. 'You've had a long day. I shouldn't have let you stay up so late.'

Mandy got to her feet. 'I wouldn't have missed seeing the mother otter and her cub for anything,' she said. She walked over to the fish box and bent down to give the cats a gentle stroke. 'Goodnight, Ferran,' she whispered.

'Don't forget you've to find names for the kittens,' Rosie reminded her.

'I'll think about that tomorrow,' promised Mandy, her eyes drooping.

It was only when Mandy had gone upstairs and was getting into bed that she remembered that she hadn't mentioned the mysterious person in the trees to Rosie.

She pulled her quilt round her and snuggled down. 'I'll think about that tomorrow too,' Mandy murmured to herself as her eyes closed in sleep.

Four

Mandy woke early the next morning in spite of the long journey and late night the day before. Outside, the sun was shining on the sparkling loch. It was going to be a perfect day.

She dressed quickly and ran downstairs.

Rosie was sitting on the floor, playing with the kittens. 'How did you sleep?' she asked, looking up.

'Like a log,' Mandy replied, getting down beside her.

Rosie disengaged a tiny bundle of fur from her T-shirt. The kitten's little claws clung to her and Rosie scolded it gently. 'This one is the boss already,' she laughed, looking affectionately at the black-and-white kitten. 'Look how his tail is twitching.'

Mandy laughed too and took the kitten from her. 'You're *so* fierce,' she joked, holding the kitten's face close to her own.

The other kittens were scrambling around the floor, butting one another and chasing their tails while Ferran looked on calmly.

'Wagtails twitch their tails like that,' said James, coming in through the front door. 'I've just seen one over by the stream. I can't believe how many birds there are here.'

'You're up early,' said Mandy.

James grinned. 'We've got to go for the milk and bread before we get any breakfast.'

Rosie looked guilty. 'I'm afraid I gave the last of it to the kittens,' she apologised. 'They're taking bread soaked in milk now.'

'Oh, *that*'s all right,' said Mandy as she watched another of the kittens scamper towards James, stop, and scamper back again towards its mother. 'We don't mind the kittens having our breakfast.'

'That's what ringed plovers do at the water's edge,' commented James, looking at the scampering kitten.

Mandy remembered the funny little birds that

didn't like to get their feet wet. '*I* know!' she cried. 'We'll call the kittens after birds.' She scooped up the kitten as it scampered back and forth. This one was a girl. 'You can be Plover,' she said.

'And the fierce one can be Wagtail,' James suggested.

'What about the other two?' asked Mandy looking at the remaining kittens.

The other girl kitten had a white chin and a black back. The remaining one, a boy, was almost completely white except for black markings under its eyes.

'The one with the markings under its eyes can be Lapwing,' said James. He dug his bird book out of his back pocket and flicked to a page with a green-backed bird with a tuft on its head and black lines under its eyes.

'Great,' said Mandy. 'That only leaves one.'

'We can think about that on our way to get the stuff for breakfast,' said James firmly.

Mandy got up. 'OK,' she agreed. When James got hungry he sometimes grew impatient. Then she turned to Rosie. 'I forgot to tell you there was somebody in the woods last night, Rosie. Do you know who it might have been?'

Rosie frowned. 'I suppose Mr Tarrant might have arrived. What did the person look like?'

Mandy shrugged. 'I didn't actually *see* anybody but I know it wasn't an animal or anything. I called out but no one answered. Then I heard a voice.'

'What did it say?' asked Rosie.

Mandy shrugged again. 'I don't know. It sounded as if whoever it was had tripped over a tree root or something.'

Rosie looked puzzled. 'The only person I can think of is Mr Tarrant and I've never met him,' she said. 'I've only spoken to him on the phone.'

'Solving mysteries is easier on a full stomach,' James said pointedly.

Mandy gave him a shove. 'OK, I can take a hint,' she said. 'See you later, Rosie.'

'Go straight up through the woods,' advised Rosie. 'That way you'll cut off most of the track.'

Mandy and James made their way around the back of the cottage and up into the woods. Above them the trees rustled in a slight breeze. James shoved his glasses right up on his nose, watching intently for birds.

'There must be loads of animals living around here,' remarked Mandy.

James nodded. 'Foxes and pine martens. Maybe even wildcats according to Rosie.'

Mandy shivered. 'I don't think I'd like to meet a wildcat,' she said.

They came out of the trees and looked down on the loch. A big black bird took off from the loch's surface and skimmed over the water. Then it dived and reappeared a moment later with a fish in its mouth.

'*That*'s a cormorant,' Mandy declared. 'I saw one yesterday. I wonder if it's the same one.'

'Probably,' said James. 'They tend to stick to the same feeding grounds.'

Mandy grabbed his arm, squinting at the bird as it raised its head and swallowed the fish. 'White chin, black back,' she exclaimed.

James grinned. 'The last kitten,' he replied, catching her meaning. 'We'll call her Cormorant. Well done, Mandy!'

'Cormorant is an awfully big name for a tiny kitten,' said Mandy, pulling a face. 'Let's shorten it to Corrie.'

'That sounds good,' James agreed. 'That makes it Plover, Wagtail, Lapwing and Corrie.'

'There's the head of the track,' said Mandy.

'And there's our food,' said James with satisfaction.

They made their way to the top of the track where a loaf of bread and a large carton of milk were tucked into an old tin bucket.

'Great system,' said Mandy admiringly.

'Right, now for breakfast,' said James, picking up the milk and bread.

'Let's just have a peek at Ardferran House,' suggested Mandy.

'I'm *hungry*!' James protested.

'You'll live,' said Mandy, hauling him towards the road and the stone gates of Ardferran House.

The driveway was overgrown in places and curved towards the house between two rows of trees. They emerged suddenly into full sunlight and in front of them was Ardferran House.

It was a large building, built of weathered stone. There was a tower at each corner and the long upper windows had stone balconies. A flight of steps led up to the main entrance and a lawn stretched right across the front of the house to where a belt of trees began. A path ran round one side of the building and Mandy thought she caught a glimpse of sunlight shining on water in the distance. It looked as if Ardferran House backed on to the loch.

'It looks like a castle,' Mandy said as they moved towards the building and gazed at the turreted roof and great oak door.

'Not quite a castle,' said a deep voice behind them.

Mandy jumped in surprise and James whirled

round. A tall man in an open-necked shirt and cotton trousers was walking across the lawn towards them. He had a severe-looking face with bushy eyebrows and piercing blue eyes.

James blushed scarlet and Mandy bit her lip. Would he think they were trespassers?

'I'm Bill Tarrant,' the man said gruffly. 'Who are you?'

'I'm Mandy Hope and this is James Hunter,' Mandy stammered. 'We're staying with Rosie Driver at Camus Ferran.'

'We're helping her with her otter survey,' James added.

Bill Tarrant looked at them critically. 'You seem a bit young for that,' he boomed. 'Still, I suppose she knows her own business best. I must go down and see how she's getting on. So, what are you doing here?'

The question was almost barked out.

'We aren't trespassing,' Mandy protested. 'Not really. We just wanted to have a look at the house.'

Bill Tarrant frowned and then seemed to make up his mind. 'OK, why not?' he said. 'Come on, let me show you my prize possessions.'

With that, he strode off round the side of the house. Mandy and James looked at each other.

'Scary!' said James.

Mandy swallowed. 'I don't think he means to be,' she said slowly. 'He's just a bit – direct.'

'Was that the voice you heard in the woods last night?' James asked.

Mandy shook her head. 'No, his is much too deep.'

'Come on then. What are you waiting for?' Bill Tarrant boomed over his shoulder.

Mandy and James hurried after him.

Mr Tarrant led them right round the back of the house and over to a low wall at the far end of a courtyard. There was a flight of stone steps leading down. Mandy caught her breath. The steps led right down to the water. Ardferran House was built above an inlet of Loch Ferran. At the bottom of the steps there was a building jutting out over the water.

'That's the boathouse,' Bill Tarrant said. 'Do you like water sports?'

At that moment a door at the back of the house opened and a boy came out. He was wearing an old pair of jeans and a jumper. He stopped when he saw them. Mandy wondered if he was Mr Tarrant's son.

'Ah, here's Neil,' Bill Tarrant said. 'How would you like to try the jet-skis, Neil?'

The boy looked about thirteen. He had a tumble

of dark hair and dark blue eyes. As he walked towards them, Mandy could see his cheeks flush slightly. 'No, thank you, Mr Tarrant,' he replied.

He wasn't Mr Tarrant's son. Even if his words hadn't told them, his voice would have. It was soft and lilting, not at all like Bill Tarrant's bass tones.

'Neil doesn't like water sports,' Bill Tarrant informed Mandy and James. 'Between you and me I think he's a bit of a scaredy-cat.'

Mandy bit her lip and looked at Neil. His face had taken on a stubborn look but he didn't say anything.

'How about you, James?' Mr Tarrant asked, leading them down the steps and opening the boathouse door. Inside there was a motor-boat, three long, sleek speedboats and several jet-skis. 'Do you want to try jet-skiing?'

James looked quickly at Mandy. 'I think I'd be a bit scared too,' he replied and Mandy gave him a smile. 'But it must be great fun.'

'I don't know what young people are coming to,' boomed Mr Tarrant. 'They seem to spend their lives in front of the television instead of enjoying the great outdoors. Well, I'm just off to have a look at some of those islands out there. Tell your mother my guests will be arriving within the hour, Neil.'

Mandy frowned. Why would Neil tell his mother that? Who *was* Neil?

The boy flushed again. 'I'll do that, sir,' he said, perfectly politely.

Mandy looked at him in surprise. 'Sir'?

Mr Tarrant disappeared into the boathouse. In a moment he was pushing a boat out into the loch. He jumped aboard, reached forward and pulled a cord and the boat shot off across the loch, leaving a foaming wake behind it.

Mandy looked at Neil. His mouth was set, his eyes dark with anger.

'Hello,' she said. 'I'm Mandy Hope and this is James Hunter. We're staying at Ferran Cottage.'

'I know,' Neil replied.

Mandy looked at him in surprise but he didn't explain.

'Do you live here?' James asked.

Neil looked across the loch. 'I've lived on the Ardferran estate all my life. Not here. Further down the loch. Now my parents have come to Ardferran House as housekeeper and handyman. So I suppose this is my home now.'

Mandy frowned. So that was why he had called Mr Tarrant 'sir'. It seemed a bit old-fashioned.

'You don't seem very happy about it,' suggested Mandy.

James was watching the motor-boat roaring off across the loch. 'You know, maybe I *would* like to try jet-skiing some time,' he said.

Neil curled his lip. 'If you come back next year you can try the lot. Speedboats, motor-boats, water-skiing, jet-skiing. You could spend an entire holiday here at Ardferran.'

'What do you mean?' asked Mandy.

'Mr Tarrant intends to turn Ardferran into a marina and water-sports centre,' Neil replied.

'Brilliant,' cried James. 'That sounds like great fun.'

Mandy looked closely at Neil. He was clearly unhappy. 'What's wrong with water sports?' she asked. 'Why don't you like them?'

Neil looked surprised. 'It isn't the water sports I mind,' he said. 'I'd try jet-skiing as soon as anybody. But not here. Not at Ardferran.'

Why not?' asked Mandy. 'Don't you like Ardferran? I think it's beautiful.'

Neil stared at her. 'Like it?' he repeated. 'I love it.'

Then he turned on his heel and walked away, leaving Mandy and James staring at each other in puzzlement.

Five

Mandy and James found Rosie down on the beach loading charts and photographic equipment into the rowing-boat.

'We'll have a quick breakfast and then row over to Eilean Mor,' Rosie said. 'I want to take some pictures of the otters' holts and try to get some more observations done.'

'Brilliant,' replied Mandy. 'I'll put the kettle on.'

'I'll fetch our binoculars,' said James. 'Let's make it a *very* quick breakfast.'

Mandy nodded enthusiastically. She wanted to spend as much time otter-watching as possible.

'Come on, Mandy,' James shouted ten minutes

later, after they'd drunk quick cups of tea and eaten slices of buttered toast.

Mandy gave the kittens a quick cuddle. 'Don't get up to any mischief while we're gone,' she warned them.

'Close the door after you,' Rosie called as Mandy appeared. 'We don't want the kittens to get out.'

Mandy drew the door to behind her and ran down to the beach to help James shove the boat off. They were both wearing plimsolls on their bare feet so they didn't care about getting wet.

'We can let the kittens out later,' Rosie went on as Mandy got carefully into the boat. 'They're too small yet to be let loose while we're not there.'

James stepped into the boat and Rosie used an oar to push off. Then they were afloat.

'Wouldn't it be easier to use a motor-boat?' Mandy asked.

'It would,' agreed Rosie, pulling on the oars. 'But I don't want to scare off the otters.'

Mandy gazed towards the island as Rosie dipped the oars in the water. The sunlight danced on the loch and the island shimmered in the heat. 'I don't see them,' she said.

'The otters aren't there at the moment,' Rosie told her. 'I want to take the opportunity to examine their holts while they're elsewhere.'

'Do you expect them to come to the island later?' James asked.

Rosie nodded. 'They usually follow a pretty straightforward pattern so long as they aren't disturbed.'

'We won't disturb them,' Mandy promised. 'We'll do exactly as you tell us.'

'You can look for spraints first,' Rosie suggested. 'Note down where they are and how long they've been there.'

'Spraints?' enquired Mandy.

'Otter droppings,' Rosie explained. 'You can tell they're otter spraints by the fish-bones in the droppings. But the spraints aren't just a way of getting rid of waste material like most other animals. Each otter has its own scent. They leave their spraints all over their territory. It's a way of communicating with other otters.'

'You mean so that one otter can tell where another otter has been?' said James.

Rosie nodded. 'Exactly,' she said. 'Dog otters also use sprainting to warn off other dog otters. Our dog otter won't want any rivals on his patch.'

'But how do we tell how long the spraint has been there?' Mandy asked.

Rosie looked round. They were drawing up to the island's shingle beach. 'If they're very dry and grey-coloured, they've been there a long time,' she said. 'Fresh spraints are usually a dark greenish-brown. Don't worry. Once you've seen a few spraints you'll be able to judge which are the most recent.'

James hopped out of the boat into the water. Mandy followed and they pulled the boat well up on to the shore.

'Don't forget Loch Ferran is tidal,' Rosie warned. 'Some of the outlying rocks at the far end of the island are completely covered when the tide is in.'

James gave the boat an extra heave. 'We don't want the boat to float away and leave us stranded,' he said.

Rosie pointed towards a tumble of rocks not far from the shore. 'That's where we'll start. Do you see the holt?'

Mandy looked where she was pointing. The rocks had fallen from the banking, leaving a wide gap in the earth above. There was another, larger rock across the top and a few spindly trees clung to the edge of the grassy bank. The soil at the entrance to the hole had been beaten down and, as they approached it, Mandy thought she could smell fish.

'Look!' cried James. 'Prints!

'Otter prints,' Rosie agreed, bending down.

'You can follow them right up to the holt,' said

Mandy, crouching down to have a closer look. Then she saw what looked like a dark brown dropping. It had a faint, not unpleasant smell. 'Rosie, is this a spraint?'

'Well done, Mandy,' Rosie congratulated her. 'That one would be a couple of days old. You see how dry it is?'

Mandy nodded and took out her notebook, jotting down a description of the spraint and its location.

'There are more over here,' James said.

Once they knew what to look for they started finding spraints all over the place. Some were very old, grey and crumbly, but one or two were quite fresh. It looked as if the otters had been here earlier in the morning.

'Watch out for the otters' tracks too,' Rosie said. 'Look, the cubs must have been having a game here.'

Mandy looked at the jumbled marks of tiny paw prints. She closed her eyes.

'What are you doing?' asked James.

'I'm trying to imagine the baby otters playing just here,' explained Mandy.

'That's great,' Rosie said. 'That's exactly why this kind of observation is so important. You can tell a lot about otter activity from examining their tracks and spraints. Look here, what do you think this is?'

They had arrived just outside the holt. Mandy looked at the tunnel dug into the banking. It seemed very deep and the fishy smell was strong. The ground in front of the tunnel was quite flat and was covered in fish scales and bits of shell and small bones.

'Fish-bones and crab shells,' Mandy said. 'The remains of the otters' dinner.'

'Quite a few dinners by the looks of it,' James added.

Rosie set up her camera and handed Mandy a ruler. 'Just lay that across the entrance to the holt,' she said. 'That way the photograph will show how big the holt is.'

Mandy laid the ruler carefully down, repositioning it at different parts of the holt when Rosie asked her to.

Rosie also took pictures of the spraints and the food remains. Then she shoved her hair back, straightening up. 'Let's go on an otter trail,' she suggested.

'What?' said Mandy.

Rosie grinned. 'Look around you. What do you see?'

'Grass and rocks,' said Mandy, puzzled.

'And heather and bracken,' put in James.

'Little tiny sheep tracks,' Mandy added, looking at the narrow runs that criss-crossed the ground, weaving in and out of the heather.

Rosie shook her head. 'There aren't any sheep on Eilean Mor.'

'They must be otter paths,' James concluded.

Mandy looked around. 'There are loads of them,' she said. 'Some going down to the shore; others into the undergrowth.' She looked at Rosie. 'I bet if we followed the paths we would find other holts.'

'I bet we would,' Rosie agreed.

'Then let's do it,' said James.

By the time Rosie called a halt half an hour later, Mandy and James were covered in grass stains. Mandy had bits of bracken sticking in her hair and James's hands were none too clean from scrabbling through the heather, trying to find the little hidden runs that the otters used.

Mandy filled in yet another entry in her notebook. 'That's five holts so far,' she said. 'How many do they have?'

Rosie laughed. 'I don't think I've found them all.'

'I don't think anybody could ever find them all,' James remarked.

'You two might,' said Rosie. 'You're both so enthusiastic. It's great having you here to help me.

You're the best assistants anyone could have.'

'We *love* it,' declared Mandy.

Rosie looked towards the shore where the waves were gently lapping the beach and raised her head to the breeze. 'The wind has changed,' she said. 'That means the tide is on the turn. The otters often come to the island just at that point and the wind will be in the right direction for us. Come on, let's settle down to watch.'

Six

'I'm getting cramp in my foot,' said James, shifting his position half an hour later.

Mandy, James and Rosie were lying on their stomachs at the top of the banking, looking down on the shore.

Mandy laid a hand on James's arm. 'Look!' she whispered, pointing to a raft of ducks on the loch.

As they watched, the ducks changed course and paddled off in a semicircle, coming back to their original course.

'Those are mergansers,' James informed her. 'They're diving ducks. You can tell by their long, hooked bill.'

'Not the ducks,' Mandy said. 'Look! There's an otter.'

A dark shape swam through the water, its head up and its body dark and sleek.

'The mergansers change course to avoid the otters,' Rosie said. 'The otters wouldn't harm them but they're so quick in the water it's as well to get out of their way. That's the dog otter.'

'How can you tell?' asked Mandy.

'Otters are easy to tell apart,' Rosie told them. 'If you look carefully you can see differences in their colouring. The dog otter has a reddish tinge to his coat and he's usually the first to appear. I think he likes to scout out the land.' Rosie looked for a few seconds through her binoculars, then continued. 'I have rather boring, practical names for each of the otters in the study, but you two could give them nice fun names while you're observing them.'

'Mm . . . it was great fun naming the kittens,' James agreed, looking through his own binoculars.

'We can call the dog otter Redcoat,' suggested Mandy. She screwed up her eyes. 'There's more than one.'

'That's one of the mothers with a cub on her back.' Rosie pointed to a slightly smaller otter.

'It's the one I saw yesterday,' Mandy said softly. 'She has pale ears.'

'Like ear-muffs,' James joked. 'We'll call her Muff.'

'And her baby can be Muffin,' added Mandy. 'Oh, look. They're coming right towards us.'

Mandy held her breath as the otters approached the island. She could hardly believe their luck as Redcoat glided into the shore and scrambled up on to a rock. He lifted his nose in the air and looked around with quick, jerky movements. It really was as if he was scouting out the land. Then he looked behind him to where Muff and Muffin were swimming shorewards and gave a whickering sound.

'He's telling them it's all right to come

ashore,' Mandy breathed, thrilled.

Muff scrambled out of the water and deposited Muffin on a big flat rock. Redcoat gave the cub a nudge and Muffin rolled over. At once he was back on his feet and nudging Redcoat. Mandy watched, fascinated, as the big dog otter played with the tiny cub. Muff seemed perfectly happy about it and even joined in.

'I don't believe it,' Rosie whispered. 'You two have brought me luck.'

'What is it?' Mandy asked.

Rosie's face was flushed with pleasure. 'Look who's just arrived,' she said. 'I didn't even notice her. You haven't seen the other mother and her cubs yet, have you? That's her now.'

Mandy shook her head, her eyes now on the other female otter and her cubs. They were scampering along the shoreline towards Redcoat. One of the cubs was keeping up with his mother quite well but the other was tiny. The mother stopped to wait for the little one as it lolloped along the shore. Redcoat sat up at once and whickered again. Then he dived into the water and disappeared for a moment before popping up further down the shore beside the mother and cubs.

'She's beautiful,' Mandy said, gazing at the

female otter. 'Her coat looks like silk.'

'You can call her Silky,' Rosie suggested.

Mandy nodded. 'What about her cubs?'

'That's easy,' said James. 'The tiny one is brown and the other one is nearly black. They can be Brownie and Blackie.'

'Like *your* Blackie,' Mandy said.

'What did you mean about us bringing you luck?' James asked Rosie.

Rosie had her camera out and was carefully setting up a shot. 'You don't often see a whole family at once,' she told them. 'This is great. If I can get shots of them all together it'll make a wonderful cover for my report.'

'What are they doing now?' asked Mandy.

Rosie was clicking away. 'I just can't believe this,' she said. 'The mothers are trying to teach their little ones to swim. These are going to be amazing shots!'

Mandy and James watched as the otters gathered together on the big flat rock. First the mothers would leap off into the water, turning and twisting and calling to their young. The cubs hung back. Silky dived and came up with a large flounder, trying to tempt the twins into the water. Blackie leaned over and tumbled head over heels right into the loch.

Mandy gasped. 'Will he be all right?' she said anxiously.

Rosie laughed softly. 'He's an *otter*,' she reassured Mandy. 'He's made for the water.'

Blackie was paddling furiously, trying to get at the fish. Then there was a splash as Muffin took to the water. Muff dived in to join her cub and the mothers swam protectively beside their babies, diving for fish and teasing the cubs into swimming a little farther before letting them have the food. Every so often the cubs would try to climb up on to their mothers' backs but the female otters seemed determined to carry on with the swimming lesson and wouldn't let them.

'Can't the cubs catch fish yet?' asked Mandy.

Rosie shook her head. 'They can't even dive properly yet. Their coats are full of air. It gets trapped in their thick fur and makes them too buoyant to dive. It'll take a little while for them to learn. But you're very privileged to see their first swimming lesson.'

Meanwhile, Redcoat sat on the rock, head up, eyes alert, standing guard over tiny Brownie.

'Poor Brownie isn't getting anything to eat,' James said as Brownie started piping pathetically.

Redcoat looked at the little cub, gave a swift glance round and slid into the water. In a moment he was back with a fish for the little one.

'And *that*'s quite unusual too,' Rosie declared. 'Males don't usually feed cubs.'

At that moment the mothers decided swimming time was over. They paddled back to the shore beside their cubs and soon the whole family was playing on the rocks, chasing one another over the beach, rolling around in furry bundles.

'They look as if they're having a great time,' laughed Mandy.

'Otters are the most playful creatures on earth,' Rosie said. 'But, if you watch them, you'll see why it's dangerous to go too near. They bite down on one another's fur when they're playing. It doesn't hurt because they have such thick fur but they can't tell the difference between doing that to another otter and doing it to a human.'

Mandy looked puzzled. 'I thought some people kept otters as pets.'

'It has been known,' Rosie replied. 'But even otters that have been pets for years have sometimes given their owners a really nasty bite. They don't mean to. It's just their way of playing.'

'Look at Brownie!' James pointed to the little cub.

Brownie had rolled right down the shore and into the water. Immediately, Silky was after him, nudging him into the water, encouraging him to swim. Brownie tried to scramble up on her back but she shook him off and splashed farther into the water, whickering at him to follow her. Brownie hesitated, took a few steps forward and stopped again.

'Go on, Brownie,' Mandy urged. 'You'll be all right. Your mum will look after you.'

As if he had heard her, the little animal moved forward again. Then there was the roaring sound of an engine and a motor-boat swept down the loch. Brownie panicked, scrabbling furiously, trying to get back to dry land. At once Silky picked him up by the scruff of the neck and darted towards the shore. When Mandy looked at the beach the other otters had gone.

'Wow!' exclaimed James. 'They disappeared so fast.'

Rosie shook her head. 'It was the motor-boat that scared them,' she said. 'I wonder who that is.'

Mandy raised her binoculars and followed the retreating motor-boat. 'It's Mr Tarrant.'

'So what's he doing roaring around on the loch disturbing my otters?' asked Rosie.

'We heard he's going to build a water-sports centre at Ardferran,' Mandy told her. 'He's got speedboats and water-skis and jet-skis as well.'

Rosie turned a shocked face to her. 'But he can't,'

she protested. 'If he does that it'll destroy the otters' habitat. There will be no more otters at Ardferran.'

Mandy looked at Rosie. 'No more otters!'

'How come?' asked James.

Rosie's eyes were troubled. 'You've seen how timid the otters are,' she began. 'In lots of places you only see otters at night because they're so shy of people. It's so quiet here at Ardferran that the otters are quite happy to come out during the day. It's a wonderful place to study them.'

'So would they go somewhere else if Mr Tarrant started a water-sports centre?' asked Mandy.

'There aren't too many places left for them to go,' Rosie replied. 'More and more of their habitats are being polluted or given over to leisure activities. Otters need long stretches of unpolluted water for feeding and breeding. If they don't have that they die. They've already suffered terribly further south because of pesticides in the rivers. I just can't believe anybody would ruin a wonderful habitat like Ardferran. A water-sports centre! Think of the pollution! Think of the noise! The otters would never survive it.'

'You mean that if Mr Tarrant's plan goes ahead our family of otters could die?' asked Mandy, horrified.

Rosie nodded. 'They certainly couldn't remain

on Loch Ferran. I don't know where else they would go.'

'But that's terrible,' Mandy protested. 'Can't we do *anything* about it?'

Rosie's mouth set in a firm line. 'I'm certainly going to try,' she said. 'I'm going to have a word with Mr "Watersports" Tarrant!'

Seven

'Let's get back,' said Rosie, jumping to her feet.

'What about the otters?' Mandy asked.

Rosie stooped and picked up her camera. 'We won't see any more of them today, I'm afraid,' she said. 'I want to go and see Mr Tarrant straight away. This is the first I've heard about a water-sports centre. Someone's got to *talk* to him!'

Mandy thought of Bill Tarrant with his big, booming voice and confident manner. She didn't think he would make a very good listener but there was no point saying that to Rosie. Maybe she was wrong. Maybe Mr Tarrant was a decent man, but simply didn't understand the harm he would do to the otters.

James shaded his eyes and looked down the loch. 'The boat's turning,' he reported. 'It looks like he's coming back.'

'Then we'll row straight to Ardferran House,' Rosie declared. 'I want to catch Mr Tarrant while I'm good and mad.'

Rosie made for the rowing-boat with Mandy and James following. Mandy pushed off and jumped in. Rosie started to row furiously, her face intent. Mandy felt almost sorry for Mr Tarrant until she remembered his confident manner. Then she began to feel sorry for Rosie.

Halfway down the loch the motor-boat passed them, sending out a wash that rocked their little boat so that Rosie had to struggle with the oars to set it back on course.

'And I'll have a word with him about *that* as well,' said Rosie, her mouth set in a determined line.

Mr Tarrant was just coming out of the boathouse when they arrived. Rosie secured the rowing-boat to an iron ring in the jetty and called to him as he ran up the steps towards the garden.

'Rosie Driver,' he boomed when she had introduced herself. 'How are you getting on with your otters?'

'Not very well this morning,' Rosie said ominously as she got out of the boat and followed him up the steps. 'I'm afraid you scared them off the island.'

'Me?' barked Mr Tarrant, looking down at her. 'I wasn't on any islands.'

Mandy and James got out of the boat and began to mount the steps. Mandy noticed a tall man in jeans and gumboots striding down the garden towards the boathouse. It was a moment before she realised who he reminded her of – Neil. This must be Neil's father.

'You didn't need to be *on* the island,' Rosie said to Mr Tarrant. 'The noise of your engine was enough to frighten the otters.'

Bill Tarrant looked at Rosie's little rowing-boat. 'So what do you expect me to do?' he asked. 'Row about in a little thing like that? I've nothing against otters, but Ardferran is going to be a water-sports centre so they'll have to get used to it.'

'But that's just the point,' Rosie said desperately. 'If you go ahead with your plans you'll chase the otters away for good.'

'So?' said Mr Tarrant. 'The people who come to the water-sports centre won't be interested in otters.'

'But *you* should be,' Rosie protested. 'You've

got a responsibility towards them.'

Bill Tarrant looked at her in amazement. 'I might have known,' he said. 'I thought I had done you a favour letting you stay on at the cottage to do your research and now this is the thanks I get. You want me to give up a perfectly sound business venture.'

Rosie bit her lip. 'I *am* grateful you let me stay on,' she began, 'but—'

Mr Tarrant didn't let her finish. 'Then perhaps you would remember that,' he barked, 'instead of telling me what to do, and interfering in things you know nothing about.' With that he nodded to Mandy and James, turned on his heel and marched off.

Mandy looked at Rosie. She was almost in tears.

'Don't take it to heart,' the man in gumboots said. 'A lot of us in Ardferran have tried to talk to Mr Tarrant about what the water-sports centre will mean for wildlife around the loch. But he's totally focused on this project of his.'

Rosie tried to smile but she didn't make a very good job of it.

'I'm Ian Cameron,' the man said. He smiled at Mandy and James. 'You two must be the youngsters Neil was telling me about.'

'You're Neil's dad?' Mandy asked.

Mr Cameron nodded. 'Why don't you all come

up to the house and Jenny, my wife, will make you a cup of tea.' He looked kindly at Rosie. 'You look as if you could do with one.'

Rosie did smile this time. 'I certainly could,' she said. 'I feel as if a steam-roller has just gone over me.'

Ian Cameron laughed as he led them up the garden towards the back of Ardferran House. 'Bill Tarrant has that effect,' he said. 'He isn't a bad man but once he's made up his mind to do something he sticks to it.'

'It's just a pity he's made up his mind to destroy the otters' habitat,' Mandy said glumly.

'He's thinking about the water-sports side of things, not the wildlife,' Mr Cameron said. 'He isn't setting out to destroy anything. He just isn't thinking about the effect his plans will have.'

'Then he should!' James burst out. 'How would he feel if *his* life were in danger?'

'Oh, I agree,' said Mr Cameron as they reached the back door and a fair-haired woman came out. 'How about a cup of tea, Jenny?'

Neil's mother smiled. 'Sure thing,' she said, looking at Mandy and James. 'Juice for you two? You've just missed Neil. He's gone off for a walk.'

Mandy was about to accept when she remembered the kittens and Ferran. 'Maybe we'd better get back and feed the cats,' she said to Rosie. 'They've been cooped up all morning.'

'Good idea,' Rosie agreed. 'I'll have a quick cup of tea and see if I can catch Mr Tarrant again.'

James pulled a face. 'Rather you than me,' he said as Mandy explained about the kittens to Mrs Cameron.

'See you later,' Rosie called after them as they headed for the track to Camus Ferran.

Mandy and James waved goodbye and trudged down the track towards the cottage.

'I didn't realise just how badly the otters would be affected by the water-sports centre,' James said gloomily.

Mandy thought of the little family of otters out on the loch. 'Neither did I,' she said. She stopped. 'Do you think that's what's upset Neil?'

James shrugged. 'He might be annoyed just because he's had to move to Ardferran House. He might not like the idea of a lot of strangers around the place.'

'Maybe,' Mandy conceded. She paused for a moment as they reached the cottage, looking out over the loch. What was going to happen to the otters? She could hardly bear to think about it. 'Come on,' she said to James, turning away from the shining waters of the loch. 'Let's play with the kittens and cheer ourselves up.'

Ferran padded across the floor to meet them as they opened the cottage door. She was certainly glad to be let out. The kittens were close behind, tumbling over their feet and scampering after their mother.

'They're just like the otter cubs,' said Mandy as she let them out. 'I'll just get them all some milk.'

'And I need to have a wash,' groaned James. 'I'm filthy with all that crawling through the undergrowth.'

Mandy looked at her own dirty hands. She gave them a quick wash, filled two bowls with milk and went outside. Ferran was sunning herself on the grass in front of the cottage. Mandy put down the bowls of milk and the cat stretched lazily and walked over to one of them. The kittens crowded round and Mandy moved the other bowl close to them.

'There,' she reassured them. 'There's plenty for everyone. Just don't fall in.'

She sat down on the grass and watched the kittens contentedly. They thrust their pink noses deep into the milk. Plover dipped her nose in too deeply and sneezed, sending a spray of milk over the others. Wagtail drew back and hissed.

'Oh, Mr Fierce,' Mandy scolded. 'She didn't mean it, did you, Plover?'

Mandy picked Plover up and wiped the kitten's nose with the tail of her shirt. Then she put her down again. There was something wrong. One of the kittens was missing. Ferran had finished her milk and was lying, stretched out luxuriously in the sun. Wagtail and Corrie were still lapping at the bowl of milk. But where was Lapwing?

Mandy heard a squeak and turned. Lapwing was standing on a stepping stone in the middle of the stream.

'How did you get there?' Mandy cried. Lapwing was certainly the adventurous kitten.

Mandy moved forward but Lapwing sprang and leaped off the stone, cleared the stream and scampered into the woods beyond.

'Lapwing,' Mandy called, running after him. 'You'll get lost.'

It was cool and shady in the woods but Lapwing was nowhere to be seen.

Mandy called softly, bending down and making chirruping noises. Where was the little kitten?

There was a rustle of branches behind her and Mandy turned, ready to scold. 'Neil!' she exclaimed.

Neil put his fingers to his lips. He was looking at something beyond her. 'Shhh,' he said. 'Is that your kitten?'

Mandy looked where he was pointing. Lapwing

was sitting in the middle of a clearing some metres away, staring upwards. Mandy made to move but Neil drew her back.

'Look in the tree above,' he said softly. 'It's a pine marten. Don't disturb it or it might pounce on the kitten.'

Mandy felt a shiver of fear as she looked up at the pine marten perched on a branch of the tree. It was the first time she had ever seen one of these animals. The marten had a brown coat and a bushy tail. Its face was pointed and its ears small and round. Its chest fur was cream-coloured. It looked very beautiful – but its eyes were fixed on Lapwing and Mandy's breath caught in her throat. The little kitten was in danger.

Eight

'What can we do?' Mandy whispered to Neil.

'When I clap my hands, you make a dive for the kitten,' Neil said in a low voice. 'We don't want Lapwing running off in fright – just the marten.'

Mandy watched as the pine marten stepped gracefully along the branch, its attention still fixed on the kitten below. Then it sat back on its haunches, prepared to spring. It leaped straight for Lapwing.

At that moment Neil clapped his hands. The pine marten twisted in midair, changing the direction of its spring. Mandy raced for Lapwing and scooped him up. Above her, the pine marten seemed to hang in the air for a moment. Then it caught a lower branch of the tree with one forefoot, twisted up into the branches and leaped without pause to a neighbouring tree.

Lapwing struggled in Mandy's arms but Mandy didn't even notice. She was watching the pine marten. With incredible agility, it leaped from tree to tree, getting higher all the time until it disappeared amongst the sun-dappled branches.

'Wow!' she said at last. 'That was amazing.'

'They're beautiful, aren't they?' agreed Neil. 'But it could have harmed your kitten. You'd better watch out in future.'

'I will,' Mandy promised. 'Thanks, Neil. I was worried about Lapwing getting lost. I didn't expect that.'

'Pine martens will take birds or baby rabbits,' Neil explained. 'But they're very shy and easily scared off.' He reached out and took the kitten from her, examining it gently. 'He doesn't seem to be hurt. Maybe just a bit scared.'

Mandy looked at him. The sullen, stubborn look was gone and he was smiling. Mandy had an idea.

'Neil, were you in the woods farther along the shore last night? Is that how you knew we were at the cottage?'

Neil nodded. 'I often come along the shore,' he

said absently. 'I like to keep up with Fergus and Heather and Ailsa. I used to see them all the time at our other house.'

Mandy was puzzled. Rosie hadn't mentioned a family nearby but Neil's dad had talked about other people in Ardferran.

'How about a cool drink?' she said. 'Then you can meet Ferran and the other kittens.'

'Ferran?' said Neil as they walked back towards the stream and the cottage. 'That's a good name.'

'Rosie thought of it,' Mandy told him. 'She found Ferran wandering around. I don't suppose you know who she belongs to? It would be a real help. You see, Rosie has to leave at the end of the week and now we have four kittens and a cat to find homes for.'

Neil looked at her intently. 'She isn't black-and-white by any chance, is she?'

Mandy nodded. 'She is. Do you know her?'

'She belonged to the MacAndrews,' Neil said. 'They moved out of Ardferran House two months ago. They couldn't take her abroad so they gave her to Mrs MacAndrew's sister. But she lives in Oban.'

'Is that a long way away?' Mandy asked.

Neil raised his eyebrows. 'Miles! She must have made her way back. She's called Cat.'

'Cat?' Mandy pulled a face. 'That isn't a very imaginative name.'

Neil grinned. 'Short for Catriona.'

'Oh, I see,' Mandy said. 'So can you get in touch with Mrs MacAndrew's sister?'

'Mum can,' Neil said. 'But what's the point if Cat's just going to come back here again?'

'Ferran,' said Mandy.

'Hmmph,' said Neil, running a hand through his dark curly hair and looking stubborn again.

James saved them from further argument. 'Hi, Neil,' he said. 'Where have you been?' he asked, turning to Mandy.

Mandy explained. 'Neil was just on his way to visit friends but I asked him to come here for a drink first. What have we got, James?'

'There's some Coke in the fridge,' James said, and made for the cottage. 'By the way,' he turned at the door, 'Rosie was wrong. Redcoat is back on the island. So are Silky and the twins.'

Neil was looking at Mandy oddly. 'I'm not going to see friends,' he said.

'I thought you said you were,' replied Mandy.

Neil shook his head as James appeared with cans of Coke.

'Brownie and Blackie are getting more swimming

lessons,' James informed them. 'Do you want to have a look, Neil?'

Neil took the binoculars and trained them on the island where James was pointing. 'It's Fergus,' he said. 'And that's Ailsa with her twins.'

'What?' cried Mandy, choking on her Coke. 'You mean those weren't people? You were talking about the otters?'

'That's right,' said Neil. 'Fergus is the dog otter and Heather is the mother of the single cub. I first saw her scrambling through the heather. I first spotted Ailsa on an island down at the bottom of the loch.'

'We've got different names for them,' James told Neil. 'Redcoat and Muff and her cub, Muffin. Then there's Silky over there with her twins Brownie and Blackie.'

'I haven't got names for the cubs yet,' admitted Neil. 'I'll use yours.'

'All of them?' asked Mandy.

Neil shook his head. 'It'll always be Fergus and Heather and Ailsa for me,' he said. 'Like Cat.'

'Ferran,' said Mandy firmly.

James had brought out Mandy's binoculars. 'Oh, look,' she exclaimed, peering through them. 'Blackie is diving. Whoops! He's just come up again. What a good swimmer he is already.'

'Otters have webbed feet,' Neil explained. 'That helps a lot. So do their long tapered tails. The tails acts as a kind of rudder for them.'

'You know a lot about otters, don't you?' said Mandy, lowering her binoculars.

'I love them,' Neil said. 'That's why I'm so angry at Mr Tarrant. He's going to ruin Loch Ferran for the otters – and lots of the other wildlife as well. I saw a sea eagle earlier in the year and there's a pair of nesting ospreys further up the loch. They're raising a second brood at the moment because somebody stole their eggs in the spring.'

Mandy's eyes darkened with concern. She hated to hear of people doing things like that. Neil obviously felt the same. 'That's terrible,' she sympathised.

'We've just come from Ardferran House. Rosie tried to persuade Mr Tarrant to give up the idea of a watersports centre but he wouldn't listen,' James said glumly.

Neil looked downcast. 'I'm not surprised,' he said. 'A lot of people on the estate have tried to get him to change his mind. He won't listen. He's determined to go ahead.'

'That's what your dad said,' Mandy told him. 'We met your mum too. They're nice.'

Neil smiled but his eyes still looked sad. Mandy bit her lip. It must be terrible for Neil, thinking about how his home was going to change. 'Are there a lot of people on the estate?' she asked. 'We haven't seen *any*.'

Neil looked up. 'I don't suppose you'd think there were many,' he said. 'You probably come from a town. There are fifteen families scattered around Ardferran. There's a school further up the lochside and a church.'

'We don't come from a town,' James replied. 'We come from a village in Yorkshire called Welford. And Mandy's parents are the local vets.'

Neil's eyes lit up. 'So you really *must* think animals are important, too,' he said eagerly.

'Of course we do,' Mandy said. 'We'd do anything to save the otters.'

'I didn't realise,' said Neil. 'Sorry if I was a bit rude to you. I didn't think you'd understand.'

'That's all right,' said James. 'We've got it sorted out now.'

'But we've got to think of some way to stop Mr Tarrant,' Mandy said. She looked out over the loch, her face gloomy. Then she smiled in spite of her worry. 'Look! Now Brownie is in the water.'

The little otter cub was swimming valiantly, bobbing up and down on the water. His mother swam alongside him, keeping a wary eye on her little cub.

'Where?' said James, raising the binoculars to his eyes. 'Oh, he's swimming. At last! Go for it, Brownie!'

'Oops!' said Mandy, giggling as a wave lifted Brownie up and deposited him neatly on his mother's back. 'He's got a piggy-back from Mum!'

The mother otter immediately shrugged her cub off into the water.

'She's determined to make him swim for it,' laughed James.

'But she's keeping close by just in case,' Mandy said.

'Look how she's circling him. Come on, Brownie. You can do it. You can swim.'

Mandy and James gazed in fascination as the swimming lesson progressed. Redcoat appeared suddenly, popping out of the water directly under Brownie. The cub paddled furiously, trying to get out of the way but Redcoat wanted to play. Up and down Redcoat went, disappearing beneath the water then reappearing under Brownie's nose, sometimes lifting the little cub right up out of the water, sometimes grabbing him by his thick fur.

'Look!' cried James. 'Redcoat is giving him a diving lesson.'

As they watched, the bigger otter rolled the cub right round and both of them disappeared beneath the surface of the water.

'Where's he gone?' shouted Mandy.

Silky swam calmly towards the spot where the other two had disappeared and dived. In a moment there was a flurry of water and all three otters appeared again, rolling and diving in the water.

'He's done it,' cried Mandy. 'He's diving. Clever little Brownie!'

Mandy and James were so intent on the playing otters that they jumped when Neil spoke.

'Oh, no,' he said urgently.

'What?' said James, swinging round.

Neil's face was serious. 'Here comes trouble,' he said, pointing down the loch.

Mandy looked where Neil was pointing. There were three white dots travelling fast across the surface of the loch. They were coming from the direction of Ardferran House.

'Speedboats,' said Neil. 'With water-skiers. Those are Mr Tarrant's guests. They're here to try out the loch.'

'Maybe it won't be suitable,' said Mandy hopefully.

'That's the trouble,' said Neil. 'A long sea loch like Loch Ferran is perfect for watersports.' He jumped to his feet, straining towards the island as the speedboats came nearer. The roar of the engines was louder now, the wake from the boats foaming white against the loch's surface. Behind the boats, sprays of water shot up from the water-skis. As they watched, the boats took a wide turn and began to head for Eilean Mor.

'Just look at the wake those boats are leaving behind them,' Neil said as a flock of oyster-catchers rose into the air and flew off. 'They'll scare the wildlife for miles around.'

'The otters!' Mandy cried, trying to focus her binoculars.

The water-skiers fanned out in a wide arc behind the boats. The boats turned, the skiers far out to the side, very near to the island. Mandy could see the wake from the boats build as it travelled fast towards Eilean Mor. The spray from the skis rose even higher as the skiers deepened into the turn. Then they doubled back on their own wake as the boats straightened out again.

'They're going,' said James.

'But look at the wash,' Neil shouted. 'It'll hit the island any moment.'

'Redcoat's on shore,' said Mandy. 'Silky's got Blackie on her back. She's heading into shore now too.'

'Where's Brownie?' cried James.

Mandy bit her lip. There was no sign of the tiny cub. The wash hit the island. Redcoat disappeared, running between the rocks. Silky followed. Where *was* Brownie?

Mandy scanned the waves as they crashed on to the island's beach. Horrified, she picked up the sight of a small brown body tumbling over and over towards the rocks on the shore. The little animal was helpless in the rush of water.

Mandy felt her heart begin to pound. It was happening already. This is what it would be like all the time when the water-sports centre opened. The speedboat's wash tossed Brownie further towards the shore. There was nothing they could do – only stand there uselessly and watch!

'He's going to hit the rocks,' Mandy gasped. Then she was on her feet, running for the boat.

'Where are you going?' James yelled.

Mandy turned for a moment. 'I'm going to find Brownie,' she said. 'That's the second time the otters have been scared off today. They won't be back. If Brownie survived that he'll be all alone.'

Neil looked at her. 'A wash like that can drown a young otter,' he said. 'Even if it didn't, he could have been thrown on to the rocks.'

'I can't see him on the beach,' James called, his binoculars to his eyes.

'He might be alive,' said Mandy. 'If there's a chance he's alive, I'm going to find him.'

'Can you row?' asked Neil.

Mandy bit her lip. 'Not very well,' she admitted.

Neil strode down the beach. 'That's OK. I've been rowing since I was five. Are you coming, James?'

'You get the boat afloat. I'll get Ferran and the kittens back into the house,' James said, turning towards the cottage.

Mandy turned briefly. 'Good thinking, James,' she said. 'But hurry. We've got to look for Brownie. He might be hurt!'

Nine

Neil rowed fast, straining at the oars, using every ounce of strength to push the boat through the water.

'Keep a look out for Brownie,' he said over his shoulder.

Mandy was perched in the bow of the boat, binoculars to her eyes, scanning the beach.

'I can't see him,' she groaned.

James was in the stern, monitoring Neil's course.

'Watch it, Neil,' he warned. 'We're heading for the wakes the speedboats left behind.'

Mandy looked at the water ahead. The wakes had spread out, leaving rising swells of water running

from the middle of the narrow loch towards the shore and the island. She grabbed the gunwale just in time. Their little boat lifted on the first swell and slid into the trough beyond. Water slapped at the sides of the rowing-boat, twisting it off course. Then the boat lifted again, perched dizzily at the top of the other swell and raced down the other side.

Neil adjusted his stroke, feathering the oars in the water. Then they were past the swells and Neil had the rowing-boat back on course.

'There's Brownie!' Mandy cried suddenly. 'I can see him.'

'Is he all right?' asked James anxiously.

Mandy turned, her eyes wet with spray. 'He's just lying on a rock,' she reported. 'He must have been thrown up by the wash. He isn't moving.'

Neil looked round, his eyes straining to see the little cub. 'Guide me in,' he shouted to James as he turned back to the oars.

'And keep watching Brownie,' James said to Mandy. 'If he *does* move we don't want to lose him.'

Neil put his shoulders to the oars and the boat sliced through the water. Mandy kept her eyes fixed on the tiny, motionless otter cub.

'OK, Neil,' James warned. 'Nearly there.'

Neil gave one last heave on the oars and the

little boat shot on to the shingle and halfway up
the beach.

Mandy leaped out and began to run, her feet
slipping on the shingle. Behind her she could hear
Neil and James dragging the boat safely up on to
the beach but her eyes were fixed on the small
brown body lying so still on a big rock farther down
the beach.

Her feet pounded on the shingle, crunching on
the pebbles and crushed shells of the beach. Then
she was at the rock, out of breath, gazing down at
Brownie.

The otter cub was sprawled across the rock, his
eyes closed, his furry little body wet from the waves.
Mandy reached out a hand and touched him gently.
He was cold. Were they too late? Then she gave
herself a shake. Of course his fur was cold from the
water. She pushed her fingers deeper into his fur.

'Please be warm,' she whispered. 'Please be alive.'

As her fingers penetrated the top layer of fur,
she drew a breath of relief. He was warm. Under
her fingers Brownie's little chest rose and fell.
Mandy dashed a hand across her eyes. She didn't
know whether she was wiping away tears or spray
but she didn't care. Brownie was alive.

'Is he . . . ?' James began, as he and Neil arrived
beside her.

'He's alive,' Mandy said. 'But I don't know if he's hurt. I can't see any blood.'

'At least the rocks here aren't sharp,' said James, looking at the flat rock Brownie was lying on.

'He's so young,' said Neil. 'That would be a help in a way.'

'How do you mean?' Mandy asked.

'His bones will still be quite pliable,' Neil explained. 'And if he was knocked out by the wave that threw him up here he would have fallen limply. That would mean less chance of any broken bones.'

'What can we do?' asked Mandy. 'I'm scared to lift him up in case we harm him.'

'We can't leave him here,' Neil pointed out. 'The other otters won't come back today and the tide is rising. This rock will soon be covered.'

'Oh, please wake up, Brownie,' Mandy pleaded. Just one little sign that the cub was all right would be enough.

Mandy stroked the cub's tiny muzzle gently. Anything would do, she thought; even a bite from those sharp little teeth. But Brownie lay still, his eyes closed. Only the slight rise and fall of his chest gave any clue that he was alive.

Neil reached over and picked up the little cub, running his hands over its body. 'I don't feel any broken bones,' he said reassuringly. 'I think the force of the wave has knocked him out.'

'Here,' offered Mandy, taking off her jumper. 'Let's at least keep him warm.'

Neil laid the little animal on the jumper as Mandy held it out. The tiny cub was small enough to hold in one hand. As Mandy carefully folded her warm jumper round him, Brownie's eyes opened at last and he looked straight at her. He drew back his lips in alarm and started making small piping noises.

Mandy gave a sigh of relief and smiled down at the little animal. 'Oh, Brownie,' she whispered on a shaky breath. 'I know you're frightened, but I'm only trying to help.'

'We'd better get him back to the cottage as soon as possible,' Neil advised.

James bit his lip. 'Rosie told us we weren't to touch the otters or interfere with them,' he reminded Mandy.

Mandy looked up, her eyes troubled. 'But if we leave him here he'll die,' she protested. 'He can't look after himself. He can't find shelter or even feed himself. This is an emergency.'

James nodded. 'You're right,' he agreed. 'I suppose we don't have any choice.'

'Let's get going then,' said Neil. 'There's no time to lose.'

* * *

Rosie was waiting on the shore when they got back. She called to them as they rowed the boat into the shallows. 'Where have you been?' she asked anxiously. 'Why did you take the boat out on your own?'

'It's all right,' James said, leaping on to the sand. 'Neil is an expert boatman.'

'Neil?' said Rosie, looking at the dark-haired boy.

'Neil Cameron.' Neil said, introducing himself tentatively.

'Oh, right! I met your mum and dad up at Ardferran House,' Rosie said.

'Did you talk to Mr Tarrant again?' James asked eagerly.

Rosie shook her head. 'He'd gone to meet his guests,' she said. 'I don't think talking to him again would have done any good anyway.'

'Probably not,' said Neil.

Rosie smiled at him. 'Your mum and dad told me you were a really keen otter-watcher.'

'He is,' said Mandy, holding her bundle carefully. 'He knows lots about otters and he saved Lapwing from a pine marten earlier on.'

Rosie looked alarmed. 'Good heavens,' she said. 'Exactly what has been going on while I've been away?'

'We'll tell you about it later,' James told her. 'We've got something to show you. Look!'

Mandy lifted a fold of her jumper and revealed Brownie. The little cub had fallen asleep, nestling in the warmth of Mandy's jumper but now he woke up and started struggling feebly.

Rosie's face grew serious. 'I thought I told you not to touch them,' she said.

'It was an emergency,' Mandy protested quickly. 'The water-skiers scared the otters off Eilean Mor and Brownie was caught up in a wave and hurled on to a rock. The other otters have gone. He was all alone.'

Rosie at once looked concerned and lifted Brownie gently out of the folds of Mandy's jumper. 'Poor little thing,' she murmured.

'We don't think he's hurt,' said Neil. 'But he isn't very happy.'

Rosie examined the cub carefully. 'He's probably just very frightened – and hungry,' she pronounced at last.

'Of course,' said Mandy. 'We'll need to feed him. But what with?'

'I'll see if he'll take some milk,' said Rosie. 'But what this little fellow really needs is some fish and there isn't any in the house.'

'What about cat food?' Mandy suggested.

Rosie shook her head. 'If we want to try and get him back into the wild we'll have to stick as closely as possible to his natural diet,' she said, looking worried. 'But where are we going to get fish? There isn't a shop for miles.'

Neil laughed. 'That isn't a problem. There's plenty of fish.'

'Where?' asked Mandy eagerly.

Neil turned and pointed at the loch. 'Out there,' he replied. 'There's a whole loch full of fish. All we have to do is catch them!'

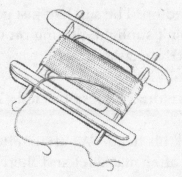

Ten

'But we don't know how to fish,' protested Mandy.

'We haven't got a fishing-rod,' James added.

Neil dug a hand into his anorak pocket and brought out an orange plastic frame with what looked like red string wrapped round it. 'You don't need a rod,' he assured them. 'A handline is good enough for mackerel.'

'But it takes ages to catch fish,' James said.

Neil smiled. 'Look!' he said, pointing to the loch. 'Didn't you notice as we were crossing back to shore?'

Mandy and James looked out towards Loch Ferran. Its surface was alive with flashes of silver.

Mandy looked up. The sun had just gone behind a cloud. It wasn't sunlight glinting on the water.

'What is it?' she asked.

'Sprats,' said Neil.

'But they're tiny,' James objected. 'Wouldn't you need a net?'

Neil shook his head. 'We aren't after sprats,' he said. 'We're after mackerel and there are loads of them out there.'

'How do you know?' asked Mandy.

'They follow the sprats and feed off them,' replied Neil. 'Whenever you see sprats you know there will be mackerel.'

'Then what are we waiting for?' said James. 'Let's go!'

Mandy looked anxiously at Brownie.

'Don't worry about him,' Rosie reassured her. 'I'll take him into the outhouse and fix up a bed for him.'

'The outhouse?' said Mandy. 'Can't he come into the cottage?'

'Not with Ferran and the kittens there,' Rosie said firmly. 'The kittens would want to play and even at this age Brownie has very sharp teeth. He might harm them. Besides, he mustn't get too used to *us* and our human scent or he won't know to stay out of the way in future.'

'Poor Brownie,' said Mandy, laying a finger on the little cub's head. 'You don't know where your mother is and now you're going to be banished to the outhouse.'

'It's for his own good,' Rosie declared. 'We have to try and return him to the island just as soon as the other otters come back.'

'I know,' said Mandy. 'But it still seems a pity.'

Brownie lifted his head and snapped at her finger. She drew it back quickly and Rosie laughed. 'I think he's getting hungry,' she warned. 'You'd better make that a quick fishing trip. Have you got something to put the fish in?'

'There's a plastic bucket in the boat,' said Mandy, running down to the boat to join James and Neil.

'Bring some fish back for Ferran and the kittens too,' Rosie called after her.

Mandy waved. 'We'll catch loads!' she shouted back, jumping into the boat as James pushed off.

'I hope so,' said James, not sounding very optimistic.

Neil pulled away from the shore. 'No problem about that,' he said as they drew out into the middle of the loch. 'Look over the side.'

Mandy looked. The water round the boat was alive with tiny, flashing silver fish. She reached down a hand and laughed as the little creatures brushed against her fingers.

'You could almost scoop them into the boat with your bare hands,' she gasped.

'I've never seen anything like this,' said James wonderingly. 'Does it happen all the time?'

Neil shook his head. 'Once in a while – at this time of year when the fish are moving to new feeding grounds.'

Neil shipped the oars and let the rowing-boat rock gently on the current. The sprats surrounded the boat like a carpet of silver.

Neil unwound the handline and handed it to Mandy. It was threaded with little hooks about a metre apart.

'What do I do?' asked Mandy.

'Just drop it over the side,' Neil advised. 'But be careful of the fish-hooks. If you get one of those stuck in your hand it can be really painful.'

'Don't you need bait?' asked James.

'Not with all these sprats around,' replied Neil. 'The mackerel are down there gobbling as fast as they can. They'll gobble the hooks up along with the sprats.'

James leaned over the side of the boat. 'Look!' he said to Mandy. 'You can see them if you peer closely; bigger fish down below the sprats.'

'There's hardly room between the sprats to see

anything,' Mandy said, dropping the line of hooks over the side. Then she peered down and saw dark shapes moving not far under the surface of the water. 'Oh, there are loads of them,' she cried. 'But why are the mackerel all here? Are they just chasing the sprats?'

Neil shaded his eyes and gazed down the loch towards the headlands that led to the sea. 'There's the answer,' he said, pointing.

Mandy and James looked. Far down the loch they could just make out a lot of black shapes in the water. They were rolling and diving, getting closer all the time.

James raised his binoculars to his eyes and looked through them. 'What are they?' he asked. 'Seals?'

'Porpoises,' Neil said. 'The mackerel follow the sprats and the porpoises follow the mackerel. The sprats end up swimming into very shallow water to get away from the mackerel. Sometimes they beach themselves and can't get back into the water. The mackerel follow and the porpoises come up the loch after them.'

'And what comes after the porpoises?' Mandy asked jokingly.

'Killer whales usually,' Neil replied.

'What?' yelled Mandy, nearly letting go of the handline. 'Isn't that dangerous?'

'Not usually,' said Neil calmly. 'And, besides, I can't see anything else out there. Just the porpoises. Keep an eye on them, James. We don't want to get too close to them.'

'Why not?' said Mandy, looking towards the black rolling shapes in the water. 'They look lovely – as if they're playing. Surely they wouldn't harm us?'

'Not intentionally,' said Neil. 'But they're after fish and if they get too near and swim under the boat then they can be a bit of a problem.'

'How come?' said James, his eyes on the porpoises.

'They're quite big,' said Neil. 'If one or two of them dive and roll under the boat they could upset us – and it isn't a good idea to be in the water with a school of hungry porpoises.'

'Ooh!' said Mandy suddenly. 'I think I've caught something. I felt a tug on the line.'

'Haul it up,' said James encouragingly.

Mandy hauled. The line was quite heavy. Mandy saw why as the hooks began to appear. She had caught three mackerel, not just one.

'My turn,' said James as he unhooked the fish.

'I'll keep an eye on the porpoises,' offered Mandy. 'I still think they're lovely.'

By the time the porpoises were getting a bit close for comfort, the plastic bucket was full of mackerel.

'Brownie will never eat all those!' declared Mandy.

'We can put some of them in the fridge for tomorrow,' James said. 'And don't forget the cats.'

'I'll gut some for you and you can have them for tea,' Neil offered. 'They're great so long as they're fresh out of the sea.'

As they headed homeward, Mandy turned to have a last look at the porpoises. The sun's warm yellow rays turned the water golden. Silver sprats, golden water and porpoises like black jewels tumbling and rolling in the water. How could Mr Tarrant destroy all this?

Eleven

Rosie came out of the outhouse as Mandy, James and Neil beached the boat.

'How is Brownie?' Mandy asked anxiously, lugging the plastic bucket of fish up the shore.

Rosie looked at the overflowing bucket and smiled. 'Hungry!' she announced. 'He'll be a lot happier when he's had some of those.'

'So he isn't hurt?' James asked.

Rosie reassured them. 'He must just have been stunned when he was thrown on to the rocks. He's as lively as ever now.'

Mandy heaved a huge sigh of relief. 'That's great,' she breathed. 'I hope he likes mackerel.'

'Show me an otter that doesn't,' said Neil, grinning.

Mandy grinned back. Neil was as pleased as they were to hear Brownie was unhurt.

'Come and see him,' urged Rosie.

They followed Rosie into the outhouse. She had made up a bed for Brownie in the corner.

'Another fish box!' James exclaimed. 'They certainly come in useful.'

A small furry bundle launched itself at Mandy and she bent down at once.

'Fish, Brownie,' she said as the otter cub twitched his whiskers and tried to scramble up the side of the bucket.

'You're right, Rosie. There's nothing wrong with *him*,' laughed James.

Mandy tipped a fish out of the bucket and watched, fascinated, as Brownie took it between his tiny paws and began to eat.

'His teeth *are* sharp,' remarked James. 'Look, he's almost finished that one already.'

'He must have been really hungry or he would be much more careful with us around,' said Neil.

Mandy held out another fish and Brownie abandoned the first one and made a grab for it.

'It's almost as big as him,' said Mandy as the fish slipped from his grasp. She bent to pick it up for

him but Rosie laid a hand on her arm.

'Watch what he does,' she advised.

Mandy sat back on her heels. Brownie looked at her and then at the fish between them. Now that his hunger had been partly satisfied, he was much more wary. He took a cautious step forward and, when Mandy didn't move, took another step. Mandy held her breath. The little animal pounced on the fish suddenly, trapping it between his paws firmly. Then he bent his head and began to eat.

When he had finished, Mandy looked pleadingly at Rosie. 'Can I pick him up?' she asked.

Rosie looked at the little otter cub. He had settled down, the remains of the fish still under his paws. As they watched, his eyes began to droop.

'He's completely full up,' Rosie said, reaching across to a shelf and taking down a pair of heavy gloves. She handed them to Mandy. 'Put these on and lift him very gently into his box, Mandy. I think he'll go off to sleep now. But he'll need to be fed again before bedtime.'

'We'll do that,' James promised. 'He'll be quite warm and safe in here, won't he?'

Rosie nodded as Mandy gathered Brownie up. He opened his eyes and made a half-hearted attempt to bite her but he was already half asleep. Mandy laid him carefully in his box. At once, the little animal curled up tightly, closed his eyes completely and was fast asleep.

'He's so beautiful,' Mandy breathed. 'See you later, Brownie.'

'Do you think the other otters will come back tomorrow?' James asked as they closed the outhouse door behind them.

'I certainly hope so,' said Rosie. 'The sooner we get Brownie back to his family the better.'

Ferran and the kittens were waiting patiently behind the door when Rosie opened it.

'How did you know we had fish?' Mandy said to them as James fetched some bowls.

Ferran yawned delicately and sniffed at the bucket.

Neil selected some fish for tea while Mandy fed the cats the delicious fresh mackerel. James put the rest in the fridge.

Neil started gutting the fish. He was amazingly quick, slicing a knife through the fish, cleaning them and filleting them.

'Where did you learn to do that?' asked Mandy as Neil laid yet another fillet on the big plate Rosie had put out.

'Dad taught me,' Neil replied. 'He's got a boat. We often go out fishing. You can come one day if you like.'

'I'd love to,' said James eagerly.

'Will you stay for tea, Neil?' Rosie asked.

Neil looked at his watch. 'I'll have to go home,' he said, laying the last fish on the plate and washing his hands. 'But I'll be here first thing in the morning.' He made for the door, giving Ferran a stroke as he passed.

'Don't forget to ask your mum about Ferran,' Mandy said, following him to the door.

Neil grinned. 'You mean Cat!' he said and walked off up the track.

'We need homes for the kittens too,' James called after him.

Neil waved as he disappeared into the trees. 'I'll put the word out,' he called back.

Mandy and James spent an anxious evening worrying about Brownie. When Mr and Mrs Hope phoned, Mandy had loads to tell them and she also got a lot of advice about otters.

'But Rosie will know what to do,' Adam Hope ended as he prepared to ring off.

'Oh, she does,' said Mandy. 'I only hope the other otters haven't been scared off for good.'

'Let us know how you get on,' her dad urged.

'I will,' promised Mandy. 'I'll report in every day.'

Mandy and James fed Ferran and the kittens

before having tea, then Mandy looked in on Brownie. He was still resting peacefully.

'I'll be back in a while with more fish,' Mandy whispered to the sleeping cub.

She closed the door of the outhouse gently and looked out on to the loch. The otters were out there somewhere. She wondered where they were – what they were doing. Was Silky missing Brownie? Was she calling for her little cub, wondering where he was? Poor Silky. She *must* be missing Brownie terribly.

'He's safe, Silky,' Mandy whispered to the dark water. 'We'll keep him safe for you. Come back to the island soon.'

She only hoped the otters *would* come back to the island. Maybe they had been frightened off for good. But even if they did come back, how long would they stay there once Mr Tarrant got his water-sports centre set up? Mandy sighed. Why couldn't Mr Tarrant *see* what he was doing? Why wouldn't he listen? She laid a hand on the outhouse door.

'Tomorrow, Brownie,' she promised. 'Tomorrow we'll get you back to your family. I promise.'

Mandy and James were up early the next day to feed Brownie and check that he was all right.

The little cub was a lot livelier this morning

and Mandy was glad she was wearing heavy gloves. 'Ouch! So you want to play?' she scolded Brownie as he tried to nip her finger. Even through the gloves she could feel the sharpness of his teeth.

It was very difficult to leave him all alone in the outhouse when she had fed him but Mandy knew that Rosie was right about keeping him out of the cottage. He was, after all, a wild animal and had to go back to the wild.

Neil arrived just as they were finishing breakfast. 'Any sign of the otters?' he asked.

Mandy shook her head. 'Not so far.'

Neil looked worried. 'Mr Tarrant is taking his friends out on the loch again today,' he told her. 'I was hoping that we might catch sight of the otters before they started racing up and down in the speedboats.'

As he finished speaking Mandy heard a distant hum and went to the window. 'Too late,' she groaned. 'Here they come!'

Rosie came to stand beside her as three speedboats sped down the loch, the water-skiers fanning out behind. 'You can help me write up my notes,' she said. 'I've got a lot of material from the charts you and James made yesterday.'

'And I've got good news about Cat,' Neil said.

'Ferran,' Mandy corrected him automatically. It had become quite a game.

'Mrs MacAndrew's sister says she'd be happy for her to stay here if we can find a home for her,' Neil went on, taking no notice.

'But that means we still have to find them homes,' said James.

'Mum says we can take Cat and one of the kittens,' Neil offered.

'That's great,' said Mandy. 'Now all we have to do is find homes for the other three. Which one do you want, Neil?'

Neil bent down and let the kittens scramble over him. Wagtail hissed. Neil held out a hand, palm turned inwards and the fierce little kitten looked at it suspiciously. Then he stepped forward and sniffed. Neil turned his hand and cupped it round the kitten's chin. Boy and kitten looked at each other. Then Wagtail rubbed his little pink nose in Neil's hand and purred.

'I'll take Wagtail,' Neil decided.

'Do you think you can handle him?' said Rosie, laughing.

Neil picked Wagtail up and gave him a cuddle. Wagtail purred, then dug his sharp little claws into Neil's jumper.

'Ow!' cried Neil. 'I don't know if I *will* be able to

handle him but I'll have great fun trying.'

'Three kittens to go,' said Mandy.

Rosie picked up Plover. 'I've got really fond of this little one,' she admitted.

'Oh, Rosie, why don't you take Plover?' Mandy asked.

'I'd love to – if you think that would be all right,' said Rosie. 'She'll have to learn to live in a flat when I go back to Edinburgh so it will be quite a change for her. I hope she won't mind.'

'She's young enough to get used to it,' said James reassuringly.

'The main thing is that you really like her,' agreed Mandy.

'And she'll always remind you of Ardferran,' Neil added.

'Oh, I'll never forget Ardferran,' Rosie assured him. 'I'd like to stay here for ever. Wouldn't you, Mandy?'

Mandy put her head on one side. 'It *is* lovely,' she said. 'And I *would* like to come back. But I couldn't imagine living anywhere but Welford.'

'Or Animal Ark,' James put in. 'What would all the Welford animals do without her?'

Mandy grinned. 'Only two kittens left, then,' she said.

'We're doing quite well,' said James.

Mandy scooped up Lapwing and Corrie. 'We'll find somewhere for you,' she promised.

'No problem,' James said. 'We've still got four days.'

Four days to find homes for two kittens. It was quite a tall order but Mandy's first worry was Brownie. She gazed out at the loch. There was no chance of the otters coming back today. The waters of the loch were churning with the wakes from the three speedboats. Mandy sighed. She only hoped Silky wouldn't forget about Brownie in the meantime.

Mandy, Neil and James spent the day helping Rosie with her notes and charts. First they collated all the data from the tracking charts that showed the otters' movements along the loch, then they cross-referenced it with the feeding pattern tables. Rosie had been keeping records of the otters' diet ever since she'd arrived at Ardferran. Mandy soon began to see just how much territory a family of otters needed to feed themselves.

'It's only when you see it all organised that you realise each group needs a huge area to itself,' said James.

Mandy nodded. 'No wonder otters are scarce,'

she said, looking serious. 'They *need* places like Ardferran!'

'There aren't too many places like Ardferran left,' Neil remarked. 'That's why an area like this is so important to wildlife.'

Mandy frowned. 'Have you tried showing your research to Mr Tarrant?' she asked Rosie.

Rosie shrugged. 'You heard him. He doesn't want to know,' she replied. 'He seems to think there's plenty of room for humans *and* animals in Ardferran.'

'Huh!' said James. 'There won't *be* any animals if he isn't careful.'

'I wonder if he knows that,' Mandy wondered.

'He's been told often enough,' said Neil shortly.

Mandy nodded. 'But it isn't the same as seeing it for yourself, is it?' she asked.

'All he has to do is open his eyes,' snorted James. 'I mean, if he just looked around he'd see what his watersports centre would do to the place.'

'Maybe he needs somebody to *show* him,' Mandy said.

'Good luck,' said Neil. 'You'll need it.'

Mandy thought about trying to show Mr Tarrant what he was doing later as she finished feeding Brownie. It was heartbreaking to leave the little cub piping in his tiny squeaky voice for his mother and having to close the door on him.

'It seems so cruel to keep him out there,' she said to Rosie.

'It'll be worth it,' Rosie assured her. 'Just wait till you see him reunited with the others. You'll be glad you didn't handle him too much.'

Mandy nodded but she couldn't help feeling sad. If only Mr Tarrant and his friends would go home. The sound of engines went on all day. First the speedboats, then the jet-skis, then Mr Tarrant's motor-boat.

'It's bound to stop soon,' Neil said. 'Mr Tarrant's friends are going home today.'

But it was long after tea when Mandy became aware that the noise had stopped. There was one final roar. Mandy looked out of the window and saw Mr Tarrant zooming past on a jet-ski. He swerved towards Eilean Mor and swept round the island and out of sight. Mandy turned back to the tracking chart she was working on. After a while she realised she couldn't hear anything. It was the first moment of silence in the long day and it was almost as surprising as the noise had been when it first started. Mandy looked up hopefully.

'They've stopped,' said James, reading her thoughts.

Mandy crossed her fingers. 'I hope so. I hope

they aren't just having a rest.'

Mandy, James and Neil rushed outside. It was strange to hear nothing but the lapping of water on the shore and the calls of the birds.

'Thank goodness for that,' sighed Rosie. 'You three set up a watch while I finish off the paper-work. If you see any sign of the otters let me know at once.'

Mandy, James and Neil spread out and settled down with their binoculars to watch. Gradually the loch returned to normal. Ducks paddled across it, oyster-catchers appeared on the shore and, far out on the loch, a cormorant skimmed across the surface of the water and dived for fish.

The sun slid down the sky and the rising tide crept up the beach towards them. Mandy was watching a flock of mergansers, their reddish-brown heads glinting in the sun as they fished.

'They're sometimes called sawbills,' James explained. 'They chase fish underwater and catch them with the serrated edges of their bills.'

Mandy was so interested in the way the mergansers dipped their entire heads into the water to search for fish that she almost missed the movement farther out on the loch. She rubbed her eyes and peered through her binoculars. Sleek, dark shapes slid, turning and twisting, diving and rolling. They were too small for porpoises. It was the otters.

Mandy turned a shining face to James. 'They're back,' she said excitedly. 'The otters are coming back!'

Twelve

Mandy wanted to cross to the island with Brownie straight away but Rosie advised against it.

'Let's wait a little just to make sure they've settled,' she said. 'They'll still be a bit wary about returning to Eilean Mor. We don't want to scare them off.'

Mandy nodded. 'Can I bring Brownie out on to the shore?' she asked

'Of course you can,' Rosie replied. 'Just make sure the kittens are safely inside.'

Mandy ran to the outhouse and gently opened the door. The little otter cub looked up and squeaked pitifully.

'Poor Brownie,' Mandy said soothingly. 'Don't worry, you'll be back with your mother soon. And you can come and play now.'

She took the gloves from the shelf beside the door and put them on. Then she lifted the baby otter up and carried him outside. Brownie struggled a little and tried to nip her fingers but the gloves protected her.

'Come on, Brownie. Come and play,' James called.

Mandy put the cub down on the soft sand and watched while he sniffed out his surroundings. Soon he was rolling around, scampering down to the water's edge and running back when a wave splashed him. Once or twice he ventured into the water, paddling furiously as he got out of his depth.

'He won't swim away, will he?' asked James.

'Not yet,' said Rosie. 'He's still not confident enough for that. But once he's back with his family I reckon he'll be swimming around quite happily in no time.'

'Look!' Neil shouted. 'He's found a crab.'

Brownie had scrambled into a rock pool. Mandy stood up and looked. There was a large crab in the bottom of the rock pool. Brownie stretched out a tiny paw and touched it. At once the crab scuttled sideways, disappearing under a rock in a flurry of sand. Brownie darted back, startled, and began squeaking in his little piping voice again.

'That one was a bit big for you, Brownie,' Mandy said.

'He'll get the hang of it,' Rosie laughed. 'Otters are wonderful at cracking open crabs.'

'The mother otters are playing with the cubs on the shore,' James reported, looking through his binoculars. 'Redcoat is fishing. He's just caught an enormous eel.'

Rosie stood up. 'I think we might risk it now,' she said. 'It looks as if the otters are going to stay there for a while. Let's give it a try.'

'I'll get the boat launched,' Neil called.

'I'll get Brownie's box,' said James.

Mandy ran down to the rock pool and scooped Brownie up. His fur was wet against her T-shirt but she didn't care. All she cared about was getting him safely back to his family.

The sun was close to setting as they set out across the calm waters of the loch. The tide was rising but out in the middle of the loch it was only a gentle swell. Mandy looked at the baby otter in his box.

'I'm going to miss you, Brownie,' she said. 'But you've got a lot to learn about being an otter and your mother is the one to teach you. Just wait and see how pleased she'll be to have you back.'

Neil and Rosie took an oar each, dipping them carefully into the water, The boat slid almost silently towards the island. It was important not to disturb the otters.

'Uh-oh!' said James, keeping look-out from the bow of the boat.

'What's wrong?' asked Neil.

'Redcoat has just disappeared round the end of the island,' James replied. 'He's vanished behind those sharp-looking skerries.'

Mandy looked at the outlying rocks, or skerries, as they were called. They would have to be careful approaching the island from here. Skerries could be dangerous to a boat.

'What about the others?' Mandy asked, peering towards the shore.

'They're still there,' answered James. Then he frowned. 'Wait a minute. Redcoat's back. He's in a hurry. He's swimming like mad.'

Mandy looked at the otters on the shore. They were close enough now to make out the different markings. Silky was sitting up on her haunches, head turned alertly to Redcoat. The dog otter scrambled out on to the shore and made straight for his little family. At once the other otters started piping and whickering.

'Something has disturbed them,' Mandy said. 'Do you think it's us?'

Rosie shook her head, puzzled. 'It shouldn't be. They can't have seen us. Otters don't have very good sight and we haven't made any noise.'

'They might have scented us,' suggested Mandy.

'The wind is in our favour,' Neil pointed out. 'I wonder what's wrong.'

'One thing is sure,' said Rosie. 'We can't approach them directly in case we scare them away altogether. We'll have to go round the end of Eilean Mor, beach the boat and bring Brownie across the island. If we let him go just above the beach the other otters are bound to scent him.'

Neil and Rosie dipped the oars, turning the boat so that it faced the rocks at the far end of the island.

'Watch out for the skerries,' Neil warned. 'They're covered at high tide. Some of them will be underwater already. One of those could easily put a hole in a little boat like this.'

They took a wide sweep round the island, heading for the far side. Rosie and Neil concentrated on rowing. Out here, beyond the end of the island, the current was much stronger than in the sheltered water between the cottage and Eilean Mor. James had his binoculars to his eyes, still trying to track the movements of the otters onshore.

Mandy looked at the rocks scattered in the water at the end of the island. They looked very sharp and dangerous. Then she rubbed her eyes and looked harder. The boat was moving fast now, riding on the flowing tide.

'Stop!' Mandy shouted.

Neil and Rosie looked at her.

'Stop!' she said again. 'Look!' She pointed at an outlying skerry. It was surrounded by swirling water. Beside it, half-submerged, was a jet-ski. But that wasn't what Mandy was pointing at. Lying on top of the rock, motionless, was a body.

'It's Mr Tarrant!' Mandy exclaimed. 'He must have had an accident! He isn't moving – and look at the water – it's rising fast!'

Mandy was right. Even as they watched the water seemed to inch up the rock. The jet-ski rocked and settled further into the water. Mr Tarrant's left leg was hanging down into the sea. He lay spread-eagled across the rock, his face almost in the rising water.

'Those rocks are completely covered at high tide,' Neil said. 'If he's unconscious, he'll drown. His life is in danger. Just like the otters,' he added in a more thoughtful voice.

'You don't mean we should *leave* him?' said Mandy.

Neil looked shocked. 'Of course not,' he replied. 'We'll have to help him.'

James gulped. He remembered wondering how Mr Tarrant would feel if his life was in danger – and now it *was*!

'But how are we going to do that?' said James. 'I thought you said there were rocks all round there.'

Neil bit his lip. 'There are,' he admitted.

'We can keep a look-out for them,' Mandy said. 'We've got to try and rescue him. We can't just leave him there and there's no time to get help.'

Rosie nodded. 'I agree. Let's get as close as we can. We can at least try to see if we can rouse him. Maybe he could swim out to the boat if we get near enough.'

'OK,' said Neil. 'James, hang over the side of the boat and shout when you see the first rocks.'

'I'll help,' offered Mandy, making sure Brownie was safely tucked inside his box.

The cub closed his eyes sleepily and curled up contentedly in the bottom of the box. Mandy leaned over the boat and peered down into the water. It was so clear she could see well down but it was difficult to judge distance.

Rosie and Neil kept their strokes steady as they approached the scene of the accident.

'Rocks,' James warned urgently.

Rosie and Neil immediately began to reverse their stroke. Then, as the boat settled, Neil drew out an oar and slid it over the side until it touched the submerged rock, fending it off. Rosie feathered the other oar to keep the boat steady.

Mandy looked at Mr Tarrant in dismay. The jet-ski lay in the water between them and Bill Tarrant. It was half-caught on an outcrop of rock.

'Mr Tarrant,' she called. 'Wake up! Can you hear me?'

There was no response.

'What are we going to do?' asked James. 'We can't get any closer, can we?'

Neil shook his head. 'Not without putting ourselves in danger,' he said. 'I wish we could get to him. We can't do anything if we can't wake him up.'

Mandy made up her mind. 'I can get to him,' she said.

Rosie looked at her. 'How?' she asked. 'I'm not going to allow you to swim. The current is strong out here beyond the island and the water is very cold even though it is summer.'

Mandy bit her lip. 'I wouldn't have to swim far,' she said. 'It's only about ten metres. You can put a rope round me. And it makes sense for me to do the swimming. You're all heavier and stronger than me – you'd be much more use *in* the boat – to steady it, and to haul Mr Tarrant in.'

Rosie looked very worried but even she had to admit it was the most sensible plan. 'OK. Let's give it a go,' she said.

'Here,' said Neil. 'Tie the rope round your waist. Then at least we can haul you back.'

Mandy grinned and slid the rope he held out to her round her middle. Rosie made sure the knot was secure then helped Mandy up on to the gunwale.

'Are you sure about this?' she said.

Mandy nodded. 'Of course,' she said more confidently than she felt. Standing up there on the edge of the boat the sea looked dark and cold and the rocks beneath looked very sharp indeed.

Mandy took a deep breath and slid into the water. She drew in her breath sharply. The water *was* cold. Then she struck out for the skerry and Mr Tarrant.

After five strong strokes she risked lowering one foot. She couldn't feel rock underneath her yet but two more strokes did it. Gingerly she put down her feet, wincing as they met sharp rock. Mandy gritted her teeth and pushed forward through the water. She was on the skerry now, nearly at the jet-ski. She passed the damaged machine, caught on an outcrop of rock, and picked her way towards Mr Tarrant.

She turned briefly and waved at the others in the boat. 'Made it!' she called.

Then she looked down at Mr Tarrant again. His head was bleeding from a cut above his left eyebrow and his face was very pale but he was breathing. Mandy let out a sigh of relief. She hadn't realised how scared she had been.

'He's alive!' she called back and saw the relief on the others' faces.

Mandy bent and shook Mr Tarrant gently. He didn't stir. She cupped some seawater in her hands and sprinkled it on his face. He moaned.

'Mr Tarrant,' she said urgently. 'Wake up. You must wake up. You're in danger.'

Bill Tarrant's eyes opened and he looked at her groggily. 'What on earth . . . ?' he began. Then he looked around and put a hand to his head, trying to sit up. His face went deathly white and he dropped his arm.

'Where do you hurt?' asked Mandy.

Mr Tarrant clutched his right arm. 'I think my arm is broken,' he said. 'I remember now, I was rounding the island when I hit those rocks.'

'We've got to get you out of here and into the boat,' Mandy said urgently. 'The tide is rising. This rock will be covered in no time.'

Mr Tarrant sat up, his face grey with pain. 'That boat?' he said, looking at Rosie's little rowing-boat.

Mandy nodded. 'I'm afraid it's going to be difficult,' she said. 'I don't quite know how we'll manage it.'

'Is everything OK?' Neil called across from the boat.

'Mr Tarrant has a broken arm,' Mandy called back. 'I don't think he can swim.'

'We'll never get the boat close enough to pick him up,' Rosie shouted.

'I'll try from the other side of the skerry,' Neil called. 'If the rocks drop more sharply there we can get in closer.'

Mandy looked at the water lapping round her toes. 'OK, Neil,' she said. 'But hurry!'

Neil and Rosie dipped the oars and started to row. It was uncomfortable to see them rowing away from the skerry to get round the other side. Mandy just hoped the skerry *did* drop off more sharply so that the boat could get nearer. She crossed her fingers and prayed that Neil knew what he was doing.

'Neil grew up on Loch Ferran,' she said confidently to Mr Tarrant. 'He knows exactly where all the rocks are.'

Bill Tarrant smiled. He looked a little better now. 'When this is over I'm going to give you the most terrible telling-off for putting yourself at risk,' he said.

Mandy grinned in spite of her worry. 'When this is over I won't mind,' she replied.

'Mandy!' shouted a voice behind them.

Mandy whirled round. The boat was heading towards them.

James leaned over the gunwale as Neil and Rosie brought it round and slowed it. 'This is as far as we can get,' he called.

Mandy shivered. She was already very cold and the boat was still too far away.

'Untie your rope, tie one end round the rock and throw the other end to us,' Neil yelled.

Mandy did as she was asked.

Neil and Rosie hauled on the rope, drawing the boat as close as they dared.

'That's as far as we can risk,' Neil yelled. 'Can you slide along the rope?

Mandy looked at the rope. It was stretched tightly between the boat and the rock. 'Of course I can,' she said. 'But what about Mr Tarrant? His arm is broken.'

'I'll manage,' said Bill Tarrant. 'But I want to see you safe first.'

Mandy took a deep breath, laid both hands on the rope and swung herself into the water. She drew her breath in sharply. The water felt even colder. She was glad she didn't have to swim back to the boat. Then she was inching along the rope, hand over hand. Rosie and James reached out for her while Neil kept the boat steady as they hauled her over the side to safety.

Rosie ripped off her jumper and wrapped it round Mandy's shoulders. Mandy's teeth were chattering.

'Now you, Mr Tarrant,' James yelled.

There was a squeaking at Mandy's feet and she looked down. Brownie was sitting in the bottom of his box looking at her. She rubbed his warm fur, her eyes on Bill Tarrant. How was Mr Tarrant going to manage it?

Mr Tarrant grabbed the rope with one hand and swung his legs up, his useless arm folded across his chest. His feet and good arm moved in sequence as he hauled himself along the rope. Mandy thought he was going to make it until she suddenly saw his face go even whiter than it had been and he dropped from the rope like a stone and tumbled into the water.

'He's fainted!' yelled Neil.

But James was already over the side of the boat,

diving, grabbing Mr Tarrant and hauling him to the surface.

Mandy watched, her heart hammering, as James struggled with Mr Tarrant's weight. Then he managed to get his arms under Mr Tarrant's shoulders and heaved.

Rosie leaned over the boat. 'Lean right out over the other side to balance us, Mandy,' she yelled and Mandy lunged for the opposite gunwale as Rosie and Neil hauled Mr Tarrant aboard.

For a moment the little rowing-boat dipped dangerously to one side, water slopping over the gunwale and Mandy was afraid they were going to overturn. Then there was a splashing below her and James reached up both hands and began to haul on her side of the boat, dragging it back.

Mr Tarrant flopped over the other side of the boat and James made a mighty effort, heaving himself in beside Mandy.

'Well done, James,' Mandy breathed fervently.

'Well done, both of you,' Rosie echoed as Neil stripped off his jumper and made James put it on. 'Now, let's get home!'

Mandy shivered as the breeze freshened. She looked back at Eilean Mor. There was no question of trying to put Brownie ashore on the island. Mr Tarrant needed medical help. He was clearly in shock, as well as having a broken arm.

Mandy bent her head and stroked the furry little cub. 'Tomorrow, Brownie,' she said. 'You'll have to wait another day to see your mother.'

Thirteen

'I can't thank you enough,' Bill Tarrant said.

It was the following morning and Mr Tarrant was sitting in the living-room at the cottage. His arm was in plaster and he had a kitten on his lap. Mandy was cross-legged beside him. 'It was Neil that managed to get the boat close enough,' she told Mr Tarrant.

Bill Tarrant looked embarrassed. 'I'm sorry I called you a scaredy-cat, Neil,' he apologised. 'That was a very brave thing to do.'

'It was Mandy and James who jumped out of the boat,' Neil said.

Bill Tarrant laughed. 'You're *all* terrific,' he

declared, looking round. 'I wish there was some way to thank you.'

'There's no need,' said Rosie kindly.

'That's right,' James put in. 'We were just glad to get you off that skerry. The tide was coming up fast.'

Mr Tarrant looked serious. 'If it hadn't been for you I wouldn't be here now,' he said. 'Even if I had regained consciousness, I couldn't have swum against the running tide with a broken arm. You saved my life. I think I also owe you an apology for being so short with you the other day, Rosie.'

Rosie smiled. 'You've been good about letting me stay on to finish my project,' she said. 'Even though you yelled at me.'

Bill Tarrant looked embarrassed. 'Sorry about that,' he muttered. 'It seems a very worthwhile project, though I didn't know it included kittens.' He looked down at the kitten in his lap. 'This is a nice little thing. Who does he belong to?'

'It's a she and she doesn't belong to anyone yet,' sighed Mandy. 'Rosie found her mother just before she gave birth. She had four kittens.'

'I'm taking the mother cat and one of the kittens,' Neil said.

'And I'm going to adopt Plover,' said Rosie.

'So that leaves Lapwing and Corrie,' Mandy

added. 'That's Corrie on your lap.'

Mr Tarrant tickled the kitten under her chin and the little animal purred with pleasure.

Mandy looked at James and he put his head on one side. 'What do you think?' he mouthed silently.

Mandy nodded eagerly. 'Do you like kittens, Mr Tarrant?' she asked innocently.

Bill Tarrant held Corrie up and looked at her. 'I like this one,' he smiled.

'How would you like to adopt her?' asked Mandy.

Bill Tarrant put Corrie back in his lap and looked thoughtful. 'I don't know about that,' he said.

Mandy's heart sank.

'You don't think she might be lonely?' Bill Tarrant asked.

Mandy saw the twinkle in his eyes. 'She might,' she agreed.

'Which one is Lapwing?' Bill Tarrant enquired.

James scooped Lapwing up from the floor at his feet and handed him to Mr Tarrant.

'I think these two make rather a nice pair, don't you?' said Bill Tarrant.

'You'll take *both* of them?' cried Mandy. 'Oh, thank you, Mr Tarrant. That means all the kittens have homes.'

'It's the least I can do after what you did for me,' Bill Tarrant said. 'And besides, I like animals.'

Mandy had a sudden idea. 'How would you like to come with us to Eilean Mor today?' she asked. 'We're going to try and return Brownie to his family if the otters are there.'

Mr Tarrant looked pleased. 'I'd love to,' he replied. 'I'll take you all in my motor-boat.'

Neil shook his head. 'Not the motor-boat,' he insisted. 'That would scare the otters away.'

'That's how Brownie got separated from the others in the first place,' James said. 'It was the water-skiers that scared the otters off and washed poor Brownie on to the rocks.'

Mr Tarrant looked suddenly serious. 'How?' he asked. 'What happened?'

'We'll tell you later,' Rosie said from the window. 'They're back. I've just seen Redcoat and Silky.'

'Let's go then,' said James. 'We don't want to miss them.'

Bill Tarrant and Neil settled the kittens beside Ferran and followed Rosie, Mandy and James out of the cottage and down to the shore.

As they shoved the boat off, Rosie took an oar. 'I'll help you row, Neil,' she offered. 'We've got quite a boatload.'

As they pushed off from shore and Neil dipped his oar in the water, the boat shot forward.

Mr Tarrant looked at Neil. 'And to think I

thought you were a softie,' he laughed.

Neil laughed back. 'Rowing is hard work,' he said. 'But it doesn't disturb the wildlife the way engines do.'

Neil explained all about the effect of engines on the loch's wildlife as they rowed across to Eilean Mor.

'I didn't really understand that before,' Bill Tarrant spoke wonderingly. He looked around at the peaceful loch. 'Things look different when you're out here with just the sound of oars dipping and birds calling.'

'It *is* different when you can see for yourself what it's really like,' said Mandy.

Bill Tarrant nodded in agreement, his eyes still on the loch. 'I didn't listen to you either, Rosie,' he said. He looked out across the water. A heron skimmed the water not far from the boat and a raft of ducks floated lazily across the shining water. 'It's so peaceful,' he said. 'You don't realise that when you're roaring up and down the loch on jet-skis.'

Mandy and James looked at each other hopefully. Could Mr Tarrant be changing his mind?

Then they were at the island. They beached the boat some way down the shore from where the otters were playing and Mandy stepped out of the boat with Brownie in her arms.

'We'll go up the bank and into the trees,' Rosie said.

'Why not straight across the beach?' Mr Tarrant asked.

Rosie explained about otters having a very good sense of smell as they trudged up the banking and into the trees.

Mandy could see Mr Tarrant looking very interested. 'Do you think he'll change his mind?' she asked James.

James shrugged. 'I think it would take a lot to make him do that. After all, he's bought all those jet-skis and boats.'

'I suppose you're right,' said Mandy despondently. 'I just can't help hoping.'

'This is the best place,' Rosie said quietly, as they approached the edge of the trees. They were looking straight down on the beach. The otters were playing by the water's edge, rolling around and chasing one another. Redcoat scuttled into the water and the rest followed.

'The little ones can dive now,' Mandy whispered excitedly as she watched Muffin and Blackie turning somersaults in the water. 'Just look at them.'

Muffin did a back flip and disappeared, leaving

shining circles rippling on the surface of the water.

'Look at that,' said James as the little cub reappeared with an eel. Muffin lay on his back, the eel between his paws, chewing on it.

'They're wonderful,' breathed Mr Tarrant. 'I've never seen anything like this before. I suppose that's because I've always scared them away.'

'You didn't realise what you were doing,' Mandy told him.

'I *should* have realised,' Bill Tarrant replied. He looked at Brownie in his box beside Mandy. The otter cub was sitting up, very alert, sniffing the wind. 'I could have caused a very nasty accident to this little fellow.'

'But you didn't,' said Mandy. 'And now he's going back to his family.'

'I think it's just about time,' said Rosie. 'Why don't you put him down on the shore while the others are busy playing in the water, Mandy?'

'Won't I frighten them off?' asked Mandy.

'I don't think so,' Rosie said. 'Just be as quiet as you can. Leave him in a rock pool if you can.'

'Why?' asked Mandy.

'To wash off your scent,' Neil explained. 'Even his mother might not accept him if she smells human scent on him.'

Mandy nodded and crept down on to the shore

with Brownie in his box. There was a big rock pool close to the shore. Mandy bent and lifted the cub out very gently. She put him carefully into the water. Brownie looked up at her and made his usual piping noise. Then his body twisted in the water, sparkling droplets flying from his fur.

'Oh, I hope they come for you,' Mandy said softly. 'We'll wait and see that you're quite safe.'

She moved back towards the trees as quietly as she had come and lay down beside the others.

'Now what?' asked Bill Tarrant.

'Now we wait,' said Rosie.

'And hope,' added James.

They didn't have long to wait. Brownie splashed in the pool for a little while then he clambered out and sat up, piping furiously.

Silky was the first to hear him. There was a flash and a swirl of water as the mother otter turned and swam towards the shore. Almost at once the other otters were after her. Brownie's piping got louder as the otters emerged from the water. Then he was running down to the shore towards his family, tumbling and rolling into the middle of them. There was a jumble of brown and black bodies as the otters greeted the littlest one joyously, then Redcoat made for the water with his family behind him.

One by one they launched themselves into the loch, sending up showers and sprays of silver.

'He's swimming,' cried Mandy, her eyes on Brownie.

'He's diving,' Neil said. 'Look at him!'

It was true. The littlest otter swam beside his mother, arched his body and dived – and dived again. The third time he came up with a fish.

Mandy watched in delight. It was Brownie's first solo dive and she felt so proud of him. 'Aren't they beautiful?' she breathed.

'They certainly are,' agreed Mr Tarrant beside her. 'I could watch them all day. And to think my watersports centre is going to endanger them.' He looked thoughtful. 'You could have just left me on that skerry, you know. I was in danger and you risked your lives to save me.'

'We wouldn't have just left you,' said James firmly.

Mandy looked at Mr Tarrant. His eyes were fixed on the otters.

'You know, it was the otters that really saved your life,' she said. 'We were coming to return Brownie and we heard them. They were really agitated. Redcoat, the dog otter, had swum round the end of the island. He must have seen you and come back to warn the others that there was a human around.'

'We wouldn't have gone round that way if the otters hadn't been alarmed,' James added.

'So I was really rescued by the otters?' Mr Tarrant said.

'In a way,' said Neil.

Bill Tarrant took a deep breath. 'Well, I think I should return the favour,' he declared.

'What do you mean?' Rosie asked.

'They saved me,' Bill Tarrant said. 'So I'm going to save them – and all the other wildlife. I'm going to give up the idea of a watersports centre and have a wildlife centre instead.'

'You mean it?' cried Neil, his face shining.

'I certainly do,' asserted Mr Tarrant. 'And I know who I'm going to ask to be its first director – if she'll take the job.' He looked at Rosie.

'*Me?*' said Rosie. 'I'd love it!'

'That's perfect,' Mandy declared.

'You can come and visit any time you like,' Mr Tarrant said to James and Mandy. 'And Rosie doesn't have to finish her otter watch this week after all. She can carry on as long as she likes.'

'I've just thought of something,' Mandy said. 'If you stay on here, Rosie, Plover won't have to be separated from the other kittens or her mother.'

'Great,' said Neil. 'Ferran will love having all her kittens round her.'

'Ferran?' said Mandy.

Neil grinned. 'You win,' he admitted. 'After all, it is rather a good name for her.'

'The otters are going,' said James.

Mandy looked out at the loch. Far out, six sleek bodies turned and twisted through the water, rolling and diving. Mandy sighed. Only a few more days to watch them, but Mandy hoped she would return to Ardferran someday.

'Goodbye, Brownie,' she said under her breath. 'Goodbye till I see you again.'

**If you like ANIMAL ARK –
you'll love JESS THE BORDER COLLIE!
A brand new trilogy from Lucy Daniels!**

Here's an extract from Book 1, *The Arrival* . . .

'Dad!' Jenny yelled across the farmyard.

Fraser Miles turned, and, at the sight of Jenny's worried expression, strode back across the yard towards her. 'What is it?' he asked urgently.

'I don't know,' Jenny replied anxiously. 'Nell seems distressed.'

Fraser followed Jenny into the stables where the sheepdog and her new-born puppies were lying. Nell was panting now, her flanks damp and hot.

Jenny watched as her father put a hand on Nell's side. 'There's another puppy on the way,' he said. 'But I was sure that there were only four. This one must be very small.'

'Is Nell going to be all right?' Jenny asked. 'She wasn't like this with the others. What's wrong, Dad?'

Fraser Miles's face was serious. 'She must be exhausted by now,' he explained.

Jenny closed her eyes and made a wish. *Please let them both be all right*. She didn't dare to watch. Nell looked up at her with mournful eyes as she struggled to give birth to this last puppy.

'There, girl,' Jenny whispered. 'Just a little longer. Be brave.'

The collie turned her head and licked Jenny's hand. Her body shuddered, then went still. Jenny felt the breath stop in her throat.

'It's OK now,' Fraser reassured her, scooping up a little bundle into his hands. 'It's over, old girl. Just you concentrate on your other four puppies.'

Her father's words rang in Jenny's ears.

'What do you mean, Dad? The last puppy isn't dead, is it?'

Fraser looked down at her and his usually stern expression softened. 'No,' he said gently. 'He isn't dead. But he might as well be. He'll never make a working dog.'

Jenny looked at the pathetic little bundle her father was holding. It was so tiny Fraser could easily hold it in one hand. He had torn away the birth sac from the puppy's head but there was no sign of the little animal breathing. Jenny touched a finger to the puppy's body. It was warm and she could feel his heart beating under his skin.

Then, as her father removed the rest of the sac,

the puppy breathed. 'It's going to live!' she cried.

'Look, Jenny,' her father said.

For the first time, Jenny noticed what her father had already seen. The puppy's right front leg was twisted at an impossible angle. 'His leg!' she cried. 'What happened to it?'

'It must have been growing like that for some time inside the womb,' Fraser Miles explained, cutting the umbilical cord and drying the puppy with a piece of old towel.

'Oh, the poor thing,' said Jenny, gently taking the puppy in her own hands. She laid him down beside his brothers and sisters. 'There,' she encouraged him. 'You feed too.'

But the puppy was far too weak. The bigger pups scrambled over him, pushing him out of the way. Even Nell pushed him away from her.

'What's wrong?' Jenny asked. 'Why is Nell rejecting him?'

'Instinct,' her father explained. 'She knows he won't survive. Look at him. He's so weak he can hardly breathe.'

'But he *is* breathing,' Jenny insisted. 'That must mean he wants to live.'

Fraser leaned over and laid his hand on the puppy's bad leg, testing it gently. 'I'd never be able to sell him,' he said.

'I'd look after him,' Jenny protested.

'You know the rules, Jenny,' Fraser Miles answered. 'Every animal on this farm has to earn its keep. This crippled little pup could never do that.'

Jenny blinked back tears. 'What are you going to do then?' she whispered.

Fraser looked at her in real concern. 'I'll have to put him down,' he said gently. 'It's the kindest thing for him. The other puppies will crowd him out. He won't get fed. He won't even get near his mother to keep warm. At least this way he won't be in pain. He won't suffer.'

Jenny swallowed hard. She knew what her father said was true. She had lived on a farm all her life. There was no room for unproductive animals on a farm.

The little puppy moved in her hands and yawned. The tip of a tiny pink tongue licked her finger. Jenny just couldn't let him go – not just yet.

'Can I have a little while to say goodbye?' she asked.

Fraser Miles bent over Nell. 'All right,' he said. 'I'll just wait with Nell to see she's OK after that last birth.'

'Thanks, Dad,' said Jenny. 'I'll take him into the

house. It's warmer there and Nell doesn't want him here.'

She was almost at the door when her father called her. 'Remember what I said, Jenny. Don't get too attached. That puppy has to go.'

Jenny nodded and looked down at the puppy. She knew what her father said made sense. But it was too late. It was *far* too late for common sense. She had already fallen in love with this puppy.

If you'd like to read more – look out for *Jess the Border collie* in the shops from June!

ANIMAL ACTION

If you like *Animal Ark* then you'll love the RSPCA's Animal Action Club! Anyone aged 13 or under can become a member for just £5.50 a year. Join up and you can look forward to six issues of Animal Action magazine - each one is bursting with animal news, competitions, features, posters and celebrity interviews. Plus we'll send you a fantastic joining pack too!

To be really animal-friendly just complete the form – a photocopy is fine – and send it, with a cheque or postal order for £5.50 (made payable to the RSPCA), to Animal Action Club, RSPCA, Causeway, Horsham, West Sussex RH12 1HG. We'll then send you a joining pack and your first copy of *Animal Action*.

Registered charity no 219099

Don't delay, join today!

Name ....

Address ....

....

Postcode

....

Date of birth ....

Youth membership of the Royal Society for the Prevention of Cruelty to Animals

AACHOD2